THE SURVIVAL GUIDE TO
MANAGEMENT CONSULTING

HOW TO TAP INTO YOUR 360-
DEGREE WISE OWL

DEDICATION

To my mother and father, who never stopped believing in me.

To my daughter, Jessica, who is growing into an even wiser owl.

This book is for you, the reader. May it inspire you to trust yourself, embrace growth, and move forward with confidence. Keep learning, keep believing, and keep going.

TABLE OF CONTENTS

INTRODUCTION
EMBRACING THE WISE OWL
WITHIN

It was 2:00 AM, and there I sat, staring at my laptop screen, surrounded by empty coffee cups and scattered sticky notes. The client presentation was due in six hours, and something still wasn't clicking. The data was solid, and the analysis was thorough, but that elusive "so what? "insight that would make our client's eyes light up – remained just out of reach. In that moment of clarity (or perhaps caffeine-induced enlightenment), I realized that being a great management consultant isn't just about crunching numbers or creating pretty slides. It's about something far more profound: the ability to see what others miss, to understand the unspoken, and to navigate the complex maze of business challenges with both wisdom and grace.

Welcome to "The Survival Guide to Management Consulting: How to Tap into Your 360-Degree Wise Owl." If you're reading this, you're either already in the trenches of consulting, preparing to dive in, or simply curious about what makes this profession simultaneously exhilarating and challenging. Whatever brought you here, know that you're about to embark on a journey that goes beyond the typical consulting playbook.

Why the Wise Owl?

Picture an owl perched high in an ancient oak tree. What do you see? Those large, penetrating eyes can spot the most minor movement in the darkness. The ability to turn its head almost completely around, taking in every angle of its surroundings. The patience to wait for the perfect moment to act. The wisdom to learn from each hunt, each success, and each failure. This is no accident. It's precisely what we need to embody as management consultants.

The owl has been a symbol of wisdom across cultures for millennia, from Athena's companion in ancient Greece to the sage advisor in countless stories and myths. But in our context, the owl represents something more specific: the consultant who has mastered the art of 360-degree awareness and strategic insight.

Think about it: when was the last time you witnessed a truly masterful consultant at work? They seem to have an almost supernatural ability to:

- See through the fog of complex business problems
- Listen not just to what's being said but to what's left unspoken
- Navigate political landscapes with diplomatic finesse
- Deliver hard truths with empathy and grace
- Transform raw data into compelling narratives
- Build trust across all levels of an organization

These aren't just skills. They're manifestations of what I call the "360° Wise Owl" philosophy, a holistic approach to consulting that we'll explore throughout this book.

The Reality of Modern Consulting

Let's be honest: consulting isn't what it used to be. The days of showing up with a pre-packaged solution and a one-size-fits-all framework are long gone. Today's business landscape is more complex, more dynamic, and more demanding than ever before. Consider these challenges:

- **The Speed of Change**

Remember when strategic plans were set for five years? Now, we're lucky if a strategy remains relevant for 18 months. Technology, market dynamics, consumer behavior, and global events create a constant state of flux. As consultants, we need to help our clients not just adapt to change but anticipate and shape it.

I recently worked with a retail client who had spent millions on a digital transformation strategy. By the time the implementation was halfway complete, three new technologies had emerged that could potentially make their entire approach obsolete. The challenge wasn't just technical. It was about helping them develop the organizational capability to evaluate and incorporate innovations continuously.

- **The Complexity Paradox**

While businesses crave simplicity, the underlying challenges become more complex every day. Supply chains span continents, data flows are measured in Peta bytes, and stakeholder expectations have never been more diverse or demanding. Yet our job is to cut through this complexity and deliver clarity without oversimplifying.

- **The Human Element**

In our rush to embrace data-driven decision-making and artificial intelligence, it's easy to forget that business is fundamentally human. Every spreadsheet represents real people making accurate decisions that affect real lives. The most sophisticated analysis means nothing if we can't connect with the humans who need to implement our recommendations.

- **The Power of Observation**

At the heart of the Wise Owl philosophy is the art of observation—not just casual-looking but profound, intentional observation that leads to genuine insight. This is where many consultants fall short. They're so busy trying to demonstrate their expertise that they forget to observe and understand.

The Three Levels of Consulting Observation

- **Surface Observation:** This is where most consultants start and, unfortunately, where many remain. It's about seeing the obvious: financial metrics, organizational charts, process maps, and stated problems. It's necessary but insufficient.

- **Pattern Recognition:** This is where experience begins to pay off. You start to recognize patterns across industries, companies, and situations. You can connect dots that others might miss because you've seen similar patterns before. But even this isn't enough.

- **Systemic Insight:** This is where the Wise Owl truly soars. It's about understanding not just what's happening and what patterns exist but why things are the way they are. It's about seeing the invisible threads that connect seemingly unrelated issues. It's about understanding the human systems, power dynamics, and cultural factors that either enable or inhibit change.

The Adaptability Imperative

One of the most crucial lessons I've learned in my consulting career is that adaptability isn't just about changing your approach. It's about knowing when and how to change. Like our wise owl friend, we need to be able to:

- Adjust our flight path when conditions change
- Switch from broad scanning to laser focus when needed
- Adapt our communication style to different audiences

- Modify our solutions based on new information
- Change our perspective to see problems from different angles

I remember working with a manufacturing client where our initial analysis suggested a straightforward solution: streamline operations by consolidating facilities. The data supported it, the financial models were compelling, and similar approaches had worked in other industries. But something felt off.

By taking a step back and observing more carefully, channeling our inner owl, we noticed subtle but critical factors we had initially missed: the deep community ties of each facility, the unique tribal knowledge held by long-term employees, and the hidden interdependencies between seemingly independent operations. This led us to completely reimagine our approach, ultimately finding a solution that achieved the desired efficiency gains while preserving the company's cultural and social capital.

The Challenge Ahead

As you progress through this book, you'll learn specific techniques, frameworks, and approaches that will help you develop your own Wise Owl capabilities. But more importantly, you'll learn how to think about consulting in a way that goes beyond tools and techniques.

You'll discover:

- How to develop your observational skills to see what others miss
- Ways to build genuine trust with clients at all levels
- Techniques for maintaining perspective when everyone else is losing theirs
- Methods for delivering value that goes beyond the immediate project
- Strategies for managing your energy and maintaining balance in a demanding profession

But first, let's acknowledge something important: becoming a Wise Owl isn't easy. It requires:

- Patience when you want to rush to solutions
- Humility when you think you have all the answers
- Courage when you need to challenge conventional wisdom
- Empathy when you're dealing with difficult situations
- Persistence when the path forward isn't clear

The Journey Begins

Throughout this book, we'll explore real stories, practical examples, and specific techniques that will help you develop your 360-degree perspective. We'll dive deep into the challenges that every consultant faces and emerge with strategies for not just surviving but thriving in this demanding profession.

Remember, the owl doesn't just represent wisdom it represents the perfect balance of observation and action, of patience and decisiveness, of tradition and innovation. As we proceed, keep this image in mind: the wise owl, perched with perfect poise, taking in everything around it, ready to act at precisely the right moment.

In the chapters that follow, we'll explore each aspect of the Wise Owl philosophy in detail. We'll look at:

- How to develop your observational skills
- Ways to build and maintain perspective
- Techniques for navigating complex organizational dynamics
- Methods for delivering insights that drive real change
- Strategies for maintaining your well-being in a demanding profession

Your journey to becoming a 360-degree Wise Owl starts now. Let's begin by understanding that true consulting excellence isn't just about what you know. It's about how you see, think, and act. It's about developing the wisdom to know what matters most in any situation and the skill to act on that knowledge effectively.

Are you ready to spread your wings and soar? Let's begin.

PART 1: OBSERVATION & ADAPTABILITY

CHAPTER 1
OWLS AS OBSERVERS

My first significant consulting project taught me an unforgettable lesson about observation. The client, a mid-sized manufacturing company, faced a pressing challenge: declining productivity. Our team arrived armed with spreadsheets and an arsenal of standard analytical tools, ready to dissect the problem and implement tried-and-true efficiency solutions. For two weeks, we delved into production numbers, scrutinized employee schedules, and combed through equipment maintenance logs. Everything pointed to a single, glaring issue: outdated machinery.

The Revelation in the Subtleties

One evening, while working late at the facility, I observed a senior operator performing minor, deliberate adjustments to his machine. His movements were fluid and precise gestures born of years of experience. Curious, I approached him and asked about his technique. He smiled knowingly and said, "Each machine has its personality. This one needs a gentle touch in the morning, but by afternoon, you have to be firm with it."

His words were a revelation. Here was a wealth of tacit knowledge that no spreadsheet could capture. His adjustments were not anomalies; they were adaptations fine-tuned over countless hours to keep the equipment functioning despite its age. At that moment, I realized that true insight requires more than just data analysis. It demands acute observation and an openness to learning from those who live and breathe the work every day.

The Art of Professional Observation

Professional observation in consulting extends far beyond casual watching. It is a disciplined practice that combines meticulous attention to detail with a deep understanding of context. Successful consultants cultivate this skill through experience and deliberate effort, akin to an owl scanning its surroundings for subtle movements.

Early in my career, I worked with a senior consultant whose methodology left a lasting impression on me. Her approach was unconventional: during the first week of any engagement, she would immerse herself in the client's environment, silently observing. She would sit in different areas of the office, attend meetings as a passive participant, and follow the natural flow of work. This immersive approach allowed her to identify patterns and nuances that were invisible to others.

Her observations yielded insights that transformed the trajectory of our projects. In one case, she noticed that employees hesitated to use a particular software tool, not because it was inadequate but because its interface intimidated them. This detail, overlooked in initial interviews, became a cornerstone of our recommendations for improving productivity.

Seeing Beyond the Metrics

During a retail banking project, our brief focused on improving customer service metrics. The natural starting point for most consultants would have been to examine customer satisfaction scores and transaction times. However, our team decided to take a different approach: we spent days simply observing.

We watched how customers moved through the branch, interacted with staff, and how the physical layout influenced their behavior. Our observations revealed surprising patterns. During peak hours, frustrated customers often left the branch without completing their transactions. Experienced tellers had developed clever workarounds for inefficient software while newer employees struggled to keep up. The branch layout created bottlenecks that exacerbated these issues. None of these insights were captured in the available metrics, yet they were critical to understanding the root causes of the problem.

The Value of Silent Presence

There is immense power in silent presence. In the consulting world, it can be tempting to assert one's expertise early, leading with analysis and recommendations. But some of the most valuable insights emerge from stepping back and simply paying attention. This practice requires humility and patience, qualities that are often undervalued in high-pressure professional environments.

For example, in a project for a healthcare provider, our team was tasked with streamlining patient admissions. While initial data suggested inefficiencies in scheduling, our week of observation told a richer story. We saw patients growing anxious in crowded waiting areas and staff juggling multiple roles without clear protocols. The root issue wasn't scheduling alone; it was a lack of alignment between staff workflows and patient needs. Addressing this required a holistic approach, informed by what we had observed firsthand.

Observation as a Collaborative Effort

Consultants are not lone owls; the best observations often come from engaging with others. Building trust with employees at all levels of an organization is crucial. When people feel heard and respected, they share insights that are invaluable to understanding the bigger picture.

I remember working on a project for a logistics company struggling with high employee turnover. Initial interviews pointed to long hours and insufficient pay as the main drivers. However, informal conversations with warehouse staff revealed a different story. Workers felt disconnected from management, and their suggestions for operational improvements were routinely ignored. By incorporating these perspectives into our analysis, we developed recommendations that addressed not just symptoms but underlying cultural issues.

Sharpening the Observer's Eye

Like any skill, observation improves with practice. Here are some strategies that have helped me sharpen my observational abilities:

- **Rotate Your Perspective:** Spend time in different areas of the organization. Each space offers a unique view of the challenges and opportunities.
- **Focus on Interactions:** Pay attention to how people communicate—both verbally and nonverbally. Body language, tone, and even silence can reveal hidden dynamics.
- **Document Impressions Promptly:** Keep a notebook handy to capture observations in real time. Details fade quickly, and even small notes can spark significant insights later.

The Intersection of Data and Observation

Data analysis and observation are not opposing forces; they are complementary tools. Together, they create a fuller, more nuanced picture of reality. While data provides the structure, observation adds the texture, bridging the gap between numbers and lived experience.

In another project, this time for a tech start-up, our data pointed to declining user engagement. Standard recommendations to optimize the user interface and enhance features seemed obvious. However, our observations of team discussions and customer feedback sessions revealed a deeper issue: the product's value proposition was unclear.

Users didn't fully understand how the platform could meet their needs. Addressing this required strategic messaging and targeted outreach, solutions that data alone would never have suggested.

The Owl's Perspective

Owls are often associated with wisdom and keen observation, and for good reason. They can notice what others overlook, adapting their strategies to the conditions around them. As consultants, we should strive to emulate this mindset. By combining analytical rigor with thoughtful observation, we can uncover insights that drive meaningful change.

My first consulting project was more than a professional milestone; it was a turning point in my approach to problem-solving. The lesson I learned to observe profoundly and think holistically has shaped every engagement since. Like the owl, we must be ever-watchful, attuned to the subtleties that define the complex environments we seek to improve.

Developing Your Observational Skills

The journey to becoming an astute observer in consulting is both rewarding and challenging. It demands deliberate effort, persistence, and a commitment to improving with every project. Through years of practice and reflection, I've come to understand that honing observational skills is not just about watching but about truly seeing and deciphering the subtle, interconnected factors that drive outcomes in a business environment.

The Value of Time and Patience

Great observation is not an act of immediate perception but a skill cultivated over time. Early in my consulting career, I often felt compelled to produce results as quickly as possible, equating speed with competence. However, the experience taught me that meaningful insights emerge when one allows themselves the time to understand the dynamics of a situation fully.

For instance, during a project for a healthcare client, my team was tasked with improving operating room turnover times. The client expected immediate recommendations, but we chose to spend several days simply observing. Instead of rushing to conclusions, we immersed ourselves in the process. Our observations revealed that while surface-level inefficiencies occurred during room cleaning and setup, the actual delays stemmed from breakdowns in communication between departments. Surgical teams were often unaware of when rooms were ready, leading to wasted time and scheduling conflicts. This insight, gleaned through patience, allowed us to propose a communication system overhaul that significantly improved turnover rates.

Patience in observation not only ensures better solutions but also builds trust with clients. When stakeholders see a consultant's dedication to understanding their unique challenges, they are more likely to embrace recommendations. It's a simple yet profound principle: taking the time to observe saves time in the long run by addressing the right problems.

A Systematic Approach to Observation

Observation in consulting must be methodical rather than haphazard. A structured approach ensures that no critical detail is overlooked and that insights are actionable. Over the years, I've developed a framework for observation that considers three key dimensions: the physical environment, social interactions, and work processes.

Physical Environment

The physical setup of a workplace can reveal much about operational inefficiencies and opportunities for improvement. Elements such as layout, movement patterns, bottlenecks, and informal gathering spots often offer critical clues.

During a project with a manufacturing client, my team focused on observing the factory floor. At first glance, the operations appeared smooth. However, closer observation revealed that workers were walking excessive distances to access frequently used tools and materials. This unnecessary movement, while seemingly minor, added up to significant lost time for a day. By reorganizing the workspace to position essential tools closer to workstations, we improved efficiency by 15%. This case reinforced the importance of scrutinizing how physical space influences productivity.

Social Interactions

Understanding how people communicate and collaborate is another essential aspect of observation. Formal organizational charts often fail to capture the actual dynamics of decision-making and information flow within a company. Observing who talks to whom, how information is shared, and where informal power canters lie can provide invaluable insights.

For example, while working with a technology company, we observed that despite the presence of a formal matrix structure, most critical decisions occurred during informal conversations among a small group of long-standing employees. This unofficial "power circle" had an outsized influence on the company's direction. Recognizing this dynamic allowed us to design a change management strategy that engaged these key influencers, ensuring smoother implementation of new initiatives.

Work Processes

Documented procedures rarely reflect the reality of how work gets done. Observing the actual processes from start to finish can uncover discrepancies between official protocols and real-world practices. These gaps often point to opportunities for improvement.

At a financial services firm, for instance, the official process requires five levels of approval for certain transactions. On paper, this system ensured thorough oversight. In practice, however, experienced staff had developed unofficial workarounds to expedite urgent cases. These informal processes were faster and just as reliable as the formal ones. Instead of dismissing these workarounds, we incorporated their efficiency into a revised approval system that balanced speed and control, significantly enhancing overall productivity.

The Role of Empathy in Observation

Practical observation goes beyond noticing physical and procedural elements; it requires understanding the human element. Empathy allows consultants to see situations from the perspective of employees and stakeholders, fostering deeper insights.

During a retail project, we noticed a high rate of turnover among front-line staff. Initial observations suggested that workload and pay were the primary issues. However, by spending time with employees and listening to their concerns, we uncovered a deeper problem: they felt undervalued and excluded from decision-making processes. Armed with this understanding, we worked with management to create initiatives that gave employees a voice in shaping policies. The result was a dramatic improvement in morale and retention rates.

Empathy in observation not only enhances problem-solving but also strengthens relationships with clients and their teams. When people feel seen and understood, they are more willing to engage in change efforts.

Overcoming Bias in Observation

One of the most significant challenges in observation is recognizing and mitigating one's own biases. Preconceptions can cloud judgment and lead to inaccurate conclusions. To observe effectively, consultants must approach each situation with an open mind, constantly questioning their assumptions.

I learned this lesson during a project for a logistics company. Based on the client's initial description of their challenges, I assumed that inefficiencies in their delivery process stemmed from outdated technology. However, careful observation revealed a different story. The real issue lay in how drivers were incentivized. The company's bonus structure encouraged speed at the expense of accuracy, leading to frequent errors and costly redeliveries. This experience underscored the importance of suspending judgment until all relevant factors are thoroughly examined.

Tools and Techniques for Effective Observation

Incorporating the right tools and techniques can enhance the accuracy and depth of observations. While direct observation remains indispensable, supplementary methods such as time-motion studies, employee interviews, and process mapping can provide additional layers of insight.

Time-motion studies, for instance, are instrumental in environments where efficiency is critical. By analyzing how tasks are performed and the time required for each step, consultants can identify bottlenecks and suggest targeted improvements. Similarly, employee interviews offer qualitative insights that might not be apparent through observation alone. Process mapping, on the other hand, provides a visual representation of workflows, making it easier to pinpoint redundancies and inefficiencies.

The Payoff of Mastering Observational Skills

Developing strong observational skills is not merely an academic exercise; it is a practical tool that delivers tangible results. In my experience, the most successful consulting projects are those where observation forms the foundation of the solution.

By taking the time to understand the nuances of a client's operations truly, consultants can craft recommendations that are not only effective but also sustainable. Observation allows us to see beyond the obvious, uncovering root causes and enabling transformative change.

Becoming a skilled observer requires patience, structure, empathy, and a willingness to challenge one's assumptions.

These qualities, when combined with the right tools and techniques, enable consultants to deliver exceptional value to their clients. As with any skill, mastery comes with practice. The more we observe, the more adept we become at recognizing patterns, drawing insights, and making a meaningful impact.

The Power of Silent Observation

Silent observation is a skill of profound importance in consulting, yet it is often overlooked or underestimated. The ability to step back, remain quiet, and absorb what is unfolding without intervention can lead to transformative insights. Silent observation allows consultants to witness the natural dynamics of a situation, unaltered by external influence. This chapter explores the essence of silent observation, its application in real-world scenarios, and its significance in crafting actionable insights that drive success.

The Art of Watching Without Interference

At its core, silent observation is the practice of attentively watching people, processes, and interactions without immediate commentary or action. This technique requires restraint and discipline. The observer becomes a silent presence, neither interrupting the flow nor influencing the behaviors being studied. Like an owl perched high in a tree, the observer must blend into the background, allowing events to unfold naturally.

During a consulting project with a prominent retail chain, I dedicated hours to observing customers in their natural shopping environment. No interviews were conducted; no surveys were distributed. Instead, I stood unobtrusively, watching as shoppers navigated the aisles. I noticed a curious pattern: many customers would pick up an item, glance at their phones, and then return the product to the shelf. This seemingly mundane behavior sparked a deeper inquiry into online price comparisons, revealing a broader trend that ultimately shaped a highly successful price-matching strategy for the company. This outcome would not have been possible without the power of silent observation.

Mastering Focus and Patience

Silent observation demands a focused mind and a patient demeanor. The modern world often conditions us to seek quick fixes and instant results. However, the value of observation lies in its ability to uncover subtleties that might otherwise go unnoticed. This process can be likened to fishing success requires stillness, concentration, and an understanding that the rewards often come only after prolonged effort.

Consider the example of a technology start-up struggling with team dynamics. Instead of jumping into immediate problem-solving, I spent the first week quietly observing team meetings and interactions. It became evident that a few vocal individuals dominated discussions, stifling valuable input from others. These observations revealed not just the surface-level issue of unequal participation but also deeper cultural dynamics that required attention. By refraining from immediate intervention, I gained a comprehensive understanding of the situation, enabling the creation of a tailored solution that fostered inclusivity and collaboration.

From Observation to Insight

Silent observation is only the first step. The actual value lies in transforming raw observations into meaningful insights that drive actionable outcomes. This requires a systematic approach that integrates observation with critical analysis and contextual understanding.

Pattern Recognition

As hours of observation accumulate, patterns begin to emerge. Recognizing these patterns is essential to understanding underlying dynamics and recurring themes. Over time, experience across multiple industries sharpens this skill, enabling consultants to identify commonalities that transcend individual contexts.

For instance, in my work with a manufacturing company, I observed classic signs of departmental silos: limited communication, blame-shifting, and duplicated efforts. These patterns were not unique to this organization I had encountered similar issues in other settings. This familiarity allowed me to address the problem early, implementing cross-departmental initiatives to foster communication and align goals. Without silent observation, these issues might have remained hidden until they manifested as significant challenges.

Contextual Appreciation
While patterns are valuable, they must be interpreted within their specific context. A solution that works well in one environment may fail in another due to differences in culture, structure, or operational dynamics. Contextual appreciation is crucial to tailoring observations into practical strategies.

Initial observations during a project to implement best practices from a highly efficient Japanese factory to a counterpart in Brazil suggested an easy transfer of methods. However, more profound observations revealed critical cultural differences. The Japanese factory thrived on hierarchical decision-making, while the Brazilian team valued collaborative input. Recognizing these nuances was key to adapting the approach and ensuring its success in the new context.

Integration with Rigorous Analysis

Data analysis and observation complement each other. Where data provides quantifiable metrics, observation captures the human element that numbers often overlook. Together, they create a holistic understanding of the situation.

In a call center project, traditional data analysis showed low customer satisfaction scores during specific periods. At first glance, the solution seemed straightforward: increase staffing during these hours. However, silent observation revealed the genuine issue of poor knowledge transfer during shift changes. Employees struggled to seamlessly pick up where their predecessors left off, leading to frustration for both staff and customers. By combining observation with data, the root cause was addressed by redesigning the shift handover process, leading to a marked improvement in satisfaction scores.

The Role of Empathy in Observation

Empathy plays a pivotal role in silent observation. To truly understand the dynamics of a situation, one must approach it with an open mind and a genuine desire to see through the perspectives of others. Empathy enables the observer to grasp not only what is happening but also why it is happening.

In a non-profit organization I worked with, silent observation uncovered deep-seated frustration among volunteers. Their dissatisfaction stemmed not from the tasks themselves but from a lack of recognition and support. By empathizing with their experiences, the organization implemented measures to acknowledge volunteer contributions, creating a more motivated and engaged workforce. This insight emerged only because observation was approached with empathy.

Challenges and Missteps in Observation

Silent observation is not without its challenges. The observer must guard against bias and preconceived notions, which can distort interpretation. It is tempting to jump to conclusions or view situations through the lens of past experiences. However, each scenario is unique, requiring a fresh perspective.

Additionally, the act of observation itself can sometimes influence behavior. People may alter their actions when they know they are being watched, a phenomenon known as the Hawthorne effect. Mitigating this requires skillful unobtrusiveness and careful interpretation of observed behaviors.

Applying Silent Observation Across Industries

The principles of silent observation are universally applicable across industries and domains. Whether in retail, manufacturing, technology, or non-profit organizations, the ability to observe without interference uncovers insights that drive meaningful change.

In the healthcare sector, for example, silent observation revealed inefficiencies in patient flow within a hospital emergency department. Rather than immediately implementing changes, time was spent observing staff workflows, patient interactions, and bottlenecks. These observations led to the development of a streamlined triage process, reducing wait times and improving patient outcomes.

Similarly, in the education sector, silent observation of classroom dynamics uncovered barriers to effective learning. Teachers unintentionally favored vocal students, leaving quieter individuals disengaged. By addressing these dynamics, the school fostered a more inclusive environment that nurtured the potential of all students.

The Transformative Potential of Silent Observation

Silent observation is a powerful tool in the consultant's arsenal. It requires focus, patience, and empathy, but the rewards are immense. By observing without interference, consultants can uncover patterns, appreciate context, and integrate insights with rigorous analysis to craft solutions that drive meaningful change. Like the owl, the silent observer watches intently, capturing nuances that others miss. Through this practice, the ordinary becomes extraordinary, and the path to success is illuminated in ways that data alone cannot achieve.

The Challenge of Objectivity

In the world of consulting, one of the most persistent and formidable challenges we face is maintaining objectivity.

Every consultant, no matter how experienced, carries with them a collection of biases, preconceptions, and personal experiences. These mental filters can color our observations and ultimately affect the decisions and recommendations we make. For practical observation, it is essential to not only acknowledge the existence of these biases but to manage and mitigate them actively. The key lies in our ability to observe without judgment, to engage with the situation at hand in a manner that is as close to neutral as possible, and to understand that the first step in solving any problem is understanding it without interference from preconceived notions.

I learned this lesson early in my career when I was tasked with a project for a luxury retail client. Coming from a background in mass-market retail, I entered the engagement with a set of expectations, including a belief that the higher-touch service model used by the luxury brand would seem, in my eyes, inefficient. After all, I was accustomed to a different pace of business, one focused on volume, efficiency, and speed. Luxury retail, by comparison, operated on a much slower rhythm, with emphasis placed on customer experience, exclusivity, and personalization, none of which seemed to align with my fast-paced, pragmatic mindset. The luxury retail model felt like an unnecessary indulgence at the time. Still, it was only through careful, objective observation that I came to understand the importance of this approach and how crucial it was to their brand identity and the overall customer experience.

It was a humbling moment in my career, one that emphasized the critical importance of setting aside my preconceived ideas in favor of a deeper understanding. I soon realized that without objectivity, I could never fully appreciate the intricacies of the situation or provide the insight that the client was looking for.

Document Everything

The first step to ensuring objectivity in any observational process is to document everything. This may seem like a simple piece of advice, but it's often the hardest to follow. The natural inclination is to process information in real time, making quick judgments based on incomplete data. To avoid this, it's vital to make a deliberate effort to document what you observe without bias. It's essential to keep detailed notes of facts and observations, permanently separating these from your interpretations and assumptions. This distinction becomes critical when you need to reflect on your notes and analyze the situation from a more transparent, more impartial perspective.

In my experience, this discipline is essential for recognizing when personal biases may be influencing your observations. I once worked on a project where I made the mistake of jumping to conclusions based on surface-level observations. It wasn't until I revisited my notes, which were meticulously separated into pure observations and interpretations, that I began to see the problem from a different angle. This separation helped me identify where my own biases had led me astray and allowed me to correct course.

I have also learned that this practice of documentation should not be done haphazardly. It requires patience and attention to detail. When you take the time to record not just what is happening but how you feel about it, how you interpret it, and what assumptions you're making, you create an invaluable tool for self-reflection and growth. On a recent project, I maintained two separate journals one for pure observations and another for interpretations and ideas. This structure made it easier for me to track how my thoughts evolved, offering me the opportunity to question my biases and assumptions at each step. Over time, this approach helped me develop a more objective and accurate perspective of the situation.

Seek Multiple Perspectives

While documenting everything is essential for individual objectivity, it is also important to seek out multiple perspectives. Objectivity does not occur in a vacuum, and often, our own biases can be reinforced by a lack of feedback from others. The benefit of working within a team or collaborating with others is that different individuals notice different things and interpret situations in unique ways. By comparing your observations with those of others, you can build a completer and more accurate picture of the situation.

On team projects, we frequently make it a practice to compare notes at the end of each day, sharing our observations and challenging each other's assumptions. This practice not only helps us maintain objectivity, but it also frequently leads to breakthrough insights. I have seen firsthand how an individual's observations, when combined with those of others, often reveal patterns or nuances that none of us could have seen on our own. It's a collaborative process that has helped me sharpen my ability to see the big picture while also focusing on the minute details that make it whole.

This approach is important when dealing with complex or high-stakes situations. When working in isolation, it is easy to overlook key aspects or to be misled by your own biases. However, by sharing your observations and listening to the viewpoints of others, you open yourself up to new possibilities and perspectives. In my consulting career, this practice of seeking multiple perspectives has been an invaluable tool for ensuring that I maintain objectivity while also deepening my understanding of the client's challenges and needs.

The Role of Experience

Experience, while essential to any consultant's success, can also be a double-edged sword. Over time, we accumulate a wealth of knowledge and expertise that allows us to identify patterns and draw conclusions more quickly. But this wealth of experience can also lead us to become overly confident in our ability to read a situation. We may fall into the trap of assuming that every situation is similar to those we have encountered before. This tendency can limit our ability to approach new challenges with a fresh perspective and, in turn, can impede our objectivity.

When I first began consulting, I would often miss essential signals simply because I didn't know what to look for. For example, in my early projects, I would sometimes focus too heavily on surface-level data or broad trends, ignoring the finer details that would later prove to be significant. As I gained more experience, I began to develop a sharper eye for patterns whether in employee behavior, customer interaction, or market dynamics. This experience allowed me to recognize recurring themes, quickly spot potential issues, and anticipate challenges before they become full-blown problems.

However, with experience comes the danger of complacency. It is easy to rely too heavily on past lessons, assuming that the same solutions will always work for every problem. Every client and every project is unique, and each context requires careful evaluation. Over time, I've learned that the key to maintaining objectivity is not just relying on my past experiences but also being open to new ideas and ways of thinking. I've realized that while experience is essential, it is equally important to remain curious and open-minded, particularly when faced with a challenge that may appear to be entirely different from those I've encountered in the past.

Common Observational Mistakes

Throughout my years of consulting, I have encountered and observed several common mistakes that consultants often make when attempting to remain objective. These mistakes can undermine the integrity of our observations and ultimately lead us to flawed conclusions. By identifying these pitfalls and learning how to avoid them, we can improve our ability to conduct genuinely objective observations and, by extension, provide better insights and solutions.

Rushing to Conclusions

One of the most common mistakes is the tendency to rush to conclusions based on initial observations. When faced with a new challenge or problem, it is tempting to formulate a hypothesis and immediately start looking for evidence to support it. However, this approach can lead to oversimplification and, ultimately, poor decision-making. I've learned the hard way that it's essential to resist the urge to jump to conclusions and to take the time to gather enough data before forming an opinion.

On one project, our initial observations suggested that a training issue was the root cause of quality problems in a manufacturing facility. However, after further observation and deeper investigation, it became clear that the actual issue lay in the raw materials being used. The materials themselves were of inconsistent quality, and even well-trained workers struggled to meet the desired standards due to factors beyond their control. This experience taught me the importance of taking the time to observe and analyze the situation thoroughly before concluding, as initial assumptions can often be misleading.

Confirmation Bias

Another common mistake is confirmation bias, where we tend to focus on evidence that supports our pre-existing beliefs and ignore information that contradicts them. This bias can distort our observations and prevent us from seeing the complete picture. I have experienced this firsthand, especially when working with a technology company where I initially believed that their development process was too slow. I was so focused on this hypothesis that I began to interpret all of the data in a way that confirmed my initial assumption. It wasn't until I expanded my focus and looked more carefully at their decision-making processes that I realized their slower pace was actually a strategic choice designed to prevent costly mistakes. This experience underscored the importance of consciously challenging our assumptions and ensuring that we are open to alternative explanations.

Oversimplification

Finally, oversimplification is another pitfall that can undermine objectivity. Business situations are rarely straightforward, and complex problems rarely have simple causes or solutions. Yet, it is often tempting to simplify a situation in order to make it more manageable or more straightforward to solve. I've witnessed this tendency in many projects, where initial impressions led consultants to believe that the problem could be fixed with a quick fix or a simple solution. However, upon further investigation, these seemingly simple issues revealed themselves to be part of a much more complicated web of interdependencies.

The Balance Between Intuition and Objectivity

As consultants, we often find ourselves balancing intuition with objectivity. Intuition, honed through experience, can be a valuable tool when navigating complex situations. It enables us to make quick judgments when time is of the essence and can often provide an initial direction when dealing with ambiguity. However, intuition alone is not enough. It must be grounded in objective observations and supported by data. Relying solely on gut feelings can easily lead to biased decision-making, particularly when we're not aware of the biases that may be influencing our judgments.

There have been instances in my career where intuition guided me to an initial conclusion. Still, upon further analysis and more profound observation, I realized that my intuition was shaped by past experiences that didn't necessarily apply to the current situation. For example, I once worked with a retail client who was struggling with customer complaints about wait times at their checkout counters. My intuition immediately told me that the issue was likely a staffing problem and that there weren't enough employees to handle the volume of customers. However, upon further observation, I discovered that the real problem was the inefficiency of their checkout process, particularly in the way that employees were trained to handle transactions. The issue was not the number of staff but how effectively they were operating within the existing constraints.

This experience taught me that while intuition can be a helpful starting point, it must constantly be tested and refined through objective observation. By keeping an open mind and using intuition as a tool rather than a final answer, I've been able to develop a more balanced approach to problem-solving. It's about integrating both the rational and the intuitive aspects of our decision-making process, allowing each to complement the other without overwhelming the other.

The Importance of Patience in Observation

Patience is a critical aspect of maintaining objectivity, yet it is often in short supply in the fast-paced world of consulting. In our rush to deliver results and meet deadlines, we can sometimes overlook the value of taking the time to indeed observe a situation in its entirety. Patience allows us to step back and avoid the impulse to solve problems before we fully understand them. In the long run, patience in observation leads to better insights and more effective solutions.

I recall a particular project where the client was experiencing high turnover among their customer service representatives. The initial recommendation from the team was to increase wages in order to improve retention. However, I insisted on spending more time observing the work environment before making any hasty recommendations. For several weeks, I observed employee interactions, team dynamics, and the overall atmosphere in the workplace. What I discovered was that the root cause of the turnover was not low wages but rather a lack of support and recognition from management. Employees felt undervalued and overworked, and as a result, they were leaving for better opportunities elsewhere. Had I rushed to recommend a wage increase, I would have missed the deeper issue that required a cultural and managerial shift.

This experience reinforced the importance of taking the time to indeed observe and listen to what is happening on the ground. It also highlighted the value of patience in consulting patience to gather the right data, patience to understand the underlying causes of a problem, and patience to work with clients to implement lasting change.

Creating a Structured Observation Process

To overcome the challenge of objectivity, it's essential to create a structured observation process. This structure not only helps to organize our thoughts and observations but it also ensures that we remain focused on the facts rather than getting distracted by personal biases or assumptions. A structured approach provides clarity and ensures that all relevant aspects of the situation are thoroughly considered before any conclusions are drawn.

When working on a project, I typically follow a series of steps to guide my observation process. The first step is to define clear objectives for the observation what am I trying to understand or uncover? Next, I establish a framework for how I will gather and document data. This includes deciding on the key metrics to observe, the frequency of observations, and the methods of documentation. Whether through direct observation, interviews, surveys, or data analysis, it's important to have a plan in place to ensure that the process is thorough and objective.

Throughout the observation phase, I make a conscious effort to avoid jumping to conclusions or making assumptions based on initial impressions. Instead, I focus on gathering as much information as possible, allowing patterns and insights to emerge organically. This structured approach ensures that I remain objective throughout the process and that my observations are grounded in facts rather than assumptions.

The Role of Emotional Intelligence in Observation

While objectivity is critical, it's also important to acknowledge the role that emotional intelligence plays in the observation process. Emotional intelligence allows us to understand and interpret the emotions and motivations of others, which can be invaluable when observing behaviors, interactions, and dynamics in the workplace. However, emotional intelligence must also be carefully managed to prevent it from clouding our objectivity.

I once worked with a client who had a highly contentious relationship with their leadership team. The employees were visibly disengaged, and there was a palpable sense of tension in the office. My initial reaction was to sympathize with the employees, especially when I saw the frustrations they were experiencing. However, as I continued to observe, I realized that the problem was not simply a matter of poor leadership; it was a deep-seated communication issue between the teams. By using emotional intelligence to understand the underlying emotions driving the conflict, I was able to approach the situation more objectively, facilitating conversations that allowed both parties to express their concerns and work toward a resolution.

While emotional intelligence is invaluable in understanding human behavior, it must always be used in conjunction with objective observation. It's easy to let our emotions cloud our judgment, particularly when we empathize with one side of an issue. However, by acknowledging and managing our emotional responses, we can ensure that they don't interfere with our ability to remain objective and offer balanced solutions.

The Impact of Organizational Culture on Observation

Another critical factor in maintaining objectivity is understanding the impact of organizational culture on both the observed situation and the way in which observations are made. Organizational culture influences behavior, decision-making processes, and the way employees interact with one another. It's essential to consider the cultural context in which you are observing, as it can significantly affect the outcomes of your observations.

I've worked with several organizations where the cultural norms and values significantly shaped the way people behaved and interacted. For example, in one healthcare organization, there was a strong emphasis on hierarchy and respect for authority. This cultural norm affected how staff communicated and how decisions were made. Initially, I struggled to make sense of the challenges the organization was facing because I didn't fully appreciate how the cultural dynamics were influencing the situation. However, by taking the time to understand the organizational culture, I was able to observe the patterns more clearly and develop insights that addressed both the surface-level issues and the underlying cultural factors.

Understanding organizational culture is an essential aspect of maintaining objectivity in observation. It provides context for the behaviors and actions you observe, helping you to interpret them more accurately and avoid making assumptions based on your cultural norms or biases. By being mindful of the cultural dynamics at play, you can gain a deeper understanding of the situation and offer more effective recommendations.

The Evolving Nature of Objectivity in Consulting

Maintaining objectivity is not a static endeavor. As consultants, we must continually adapt and evolve in our ability to observe objectively. The business world is constantly changing, and new challenges and complexities arise with each new project. The ability to remain objective requires ongoing self-awareness, continual learning, and a commitment to refining our observational skills.

In the early stages of my consulting career, I often found it challenging to navigate the complexity of different industries and organizations. I was still developing my ability to discern between what was truly relevant and what was simply noise. Over the years, as I gained more experience and refined my approach, I became more adept at distinguishing between surface-level symptoms and the underlying issues that needed to be addressed. This

on in my observational skills has been a key factor in

my ccess as a consultant, and it has been instrumental in maintaining objectivity.

The ability to evolve and adapt is essential in the consulting profession. As we face new challenges, it's important to stay open-minded and to continually refine our skills. Whether through formal education, mentorship, or hands-on experience, we must constantly seek ways to improve our ability to observe and understand the situations we are faced with.

The Path to Effective Observation

The challenge of maintaining objectivity in observation is a constant one, but it is essential for effective consulting. By documenting everything, seeking multiple perspectives, balancing intuition with objectivity, practicing patience, creating a structured observation process, and embracing emotional intelligence, we can improve our ability to observe objectively and provide valuable insights to our clients. It is through this disciplined and intentional approach that we can uncover the true nature of the challenges our clients face and ultimately provide the most effective solutions.

Building an Observation-Based Consulting Practice

Incorporating strong observational skills into your consulting practice is not a trivial matter it requires dedication, a strategic approach, and a commitment to developing a deeper understanding of organizational dynamics. As consultants, our role is not just to provide solutions but to understand the true nature of the challenges our clients face. Often, the most powerful insights come not from data points but from what we observe during our work.

The art of observation is one of the most valuable tools in consulting, yet it is often overlooked or underestimated. To truly build an observation-based consulting practice, one must go beyond simply noticing what's happening at the surface level. The skill lies in being able to spot patterns, identify subtle dynamics, and uncover hidden insights that others may miss. This is where the value of a seasoned consultant becomes most apparent.

Allocate Time for Observation

Building a strong observation-based consulting practice begins with a deliberate investment of time. The importance of dedicating time specifically to observation cannot be overstated. This is not about rushing into a solution or coming up with a quick fix to appease clients; it's about taking the necessary time to truly understand the environment in which you're working. Observation is an active process requiring patience and a systematic approach.

In my consulting practice, I've come to insist on a minimum of three full days of observation before embarking on any significant change initiative. Though this might seem like a luxury at first glance, it is, in fact, an investment that consistently pays off. The insights gained during this time often reveal critical factors that were not immediately apparent in the initial project brief. Whether it's observing the way teams interact, how information flows through the organization or even the subtle undercurrents of office culture, this time allows me to gather a rich array of data that forms the foundation of a more effective solution.

I recognize that not every client can afford to dedicate this much time upfront. Still, I've found that even a few days of focused observation can uncover hidden pain points or reveal opportunities for improvement that would otherwise remain unnoticed. It's essential to approach these observation periods with an open mind, free of preconceived notions, and to be ready to adapt to what you discover. Clients often think they know what the issues are, but observation can provide an entirely new perspective on their challenges.

Create Observation Frameworks

While observation is a key tool in the consulting toolbox, it's only as effective as the system used to record and analyze it. To ensure that the observations you make are meaningful and actionable, it's crucial to develop a structured framework for documenting your findings. This framework serves as the foundation for turning raw data into valuable insights.

One framework that I've found particularly effective divides observations into three distinct categories: **physical flows**, **information flows**, and **emotional flows**. These categories provide a comprehensive view of the organization from multiple angles, each of which is critical to understanding the bigger picture.

- **Physical flows** refer to the movement of people, materials, and resources within an organization. This could be something as simple as how employees move through a building or how equipment is distributed across departments. Physical flow can reveal inefficiencies in space usage, logistics, or even interpersonal dynamics.

- **Information flows** focus on how knowledge and decisions move throughout the organization. Is information shared freely, or are there silos that inhibit effective communication? Are decisions made at the top and cascaded down, or is there a more collaborative, decentralized decision-making process? Understanding information flow is key to identifying communication barriers or missed opportunities for collaboration.

- **Emotional flows** are perhaps the most subtle, but they're also one of the most important. Emotional flows refer to how motivation, energy, and engagement move throughout the organization. Are employees motivated and enthusiastic, or is there a sense of disengagement and burnout? Emotional flows can often provide insight into the underlying culture of an organization, revealing attitudes and beliefs that may not be immediately apparent.

Incorporating these frameworks into your consulting practice can help you approach observations more systematically, ensuring that no critical aspect of the organization is overlooked. Each observation can be categorized and analyzed for its impact on the organization's performance, ultimately guiding you toward a more informed and effective solution.

Training Your Team

As a consulting leader, you'll likely be managing a team of consultants who are responsible for gathering and analyzing observations. To ensure the success of an observation-based practice, it's essential to invest in training your team to develop their observational skills. This doesn't mean simply instructing them to "pay attention"—it means giving them the tools and knowledge to observe effectively and interpret their findings in a meaningful way.

First, it's essential to **teach the basics** what to look for, how to document observations, and how to interpret the subtle cues that may otherwise go unnoticed. I regularly conduct workshops for junior consultants, where we dive deep into the art of observation. These workshops go beyond essential note-taking; they include practical exercises designed to teach consultants how to spot key indicators, read body language, and understand the nuances of organizational behavior.

A critical part of this training also includes **providing practice opportunities**. Like any skill, observation improves with practice, and junior consultants need to hone their ability to observe in real-world settings. On larger projects, I often assign them to spend their first few days simply observing the organization without being actively involved in the work. This "silent learning" period allows them to immerse themselves in the environment, picking up on the details they might otherwise miss. Afterward, we come together as a team to discuss their observations, providing constructive feedback and guiding them in how to interpret what they've seen.

By investing time and energy in developing the observational skills of your team, you ensure that your practice has a broader depth of insight and more diverse perspectives, ultimately leading to more comprehensive and well-rounded solutions for your clients.

The Future of Observation in Consulting

As technology advances at a rapid pace, it's natural to wonder about the relevance of human observation in an age dominated by data analytics and artificial intelligence. After all, computers can process vast amounts of information quickly, and algorithms can predict outcomes with startling accuracy. So, is human observation still necessary?

The answer, in short, is yes. In fact, I believe that as technology becomes more advanced, the role of human observation in consulting will only become more important.

While AI and data analytics excel at processing quantitative data, they cannot replicate the nuanced understanding that comes from careful human observation. Machines can analyze numbers, but they cannot interpret human behavior, understand cultural contexts, or pick up on the subtleties of emotional cues. These are qualities that remain essential in consulting, and they are often the key to understanding the deeper dynamics of an organization.

That being said, technology is not to be dismissed. **Combining traditional observation with new technologies** can yield powerful insights that would be difficult to achieve through either approach alone. For example, in retail environments, video analysis tools can support human observation by tracking customer behavior and identifying trends that might not be immediately obvious. In manufacturing, sensors that measure equipment performance can be combined with personal observation to gain a fuller understanding of operational efficiency.

The future of consulting will involve finding ways to **merge the human element of observation with technological tools** to create richer, more actionable insights. This combination holds the potential to revolutionize the way we approach problem-solving and client service.

Observation as a Cornerstone of Consulting

Ultimately, the skill of observation is central to the success of any consulting practice. As consultants, we must learn to develop keen senses, like the owl, who can see clearly even in the darkness. Observation is not a passive act; it requires active engagement, patience, and a willingness to understand what lies beneath the surface. When coupled with structured frameworks, trained teams, and technological tools, observation becomes a powerful force for change and innovation.

The journey to mastering observation takes time, but it is well worth the effort. When you commit to observing, watching what others miss, and understanding the subtle cues around you, you'll find that the insights you gain can guide your clients toward better, more sustainable solutions. In the world of consulting, your ability to observe effectively can set you apart from others and ultimately shape the future of the organizations you work with.

CHAPTER 2
ADAPTATION IN THE WILD

T he sun was sinking low, casting long shadows across Singapore's skyline as I sat in a conference room, facing a challenge that would test everything I knew about consulting. My client, a traditional manufacturing company, was struggling to keep pace with the tech start-ups that were rapidly revolutionizing their industry. Their executive team sat before me, their faces a mixture of concern and anticipation as they waited for solutions. The pressure was palpable. In that moment, I remembered an experience from my childhood, a memory that would help shape my approach.

It was a summer evening, and I had been sitting quietly near the edge of a forested area near my home. The air was thick with the sounds of crickets, the earth warm beneath me. Suddenly, a large owl glided overhead, its wings silent in the twilight. I marveled at how effortlessly it shifted from hunting in broad daylight to seamlessly continuing its pursuit in the dark. The owl's flight was not merely about survival;

it was a demonstration of evolution in motion, of adapting to the changing environment. I reflected on that moment, understanding that adaptation was not just about reacting to change but thriving within it.

The Nature of Adaptation

Throughout my fifteen years in consulting, I have witnessed countless businesses struggle with change. Some resist it, clinging desperately to the familiar until the weight of their inertia drags them down. Others fall into the trap of chasing every fleeting trend, abandoning their core principles in the pursuit of something that promises quick rewards but ultimately leaves them lost. The rare few the ones that thrive are those who learn to adapt not in a reactive frenzy but with thoughtfulness, intent, and purpose.

Adaptation is a balancing act, and it goes beyond simply embracing the next shiny object in the market. Proper adaptation involves understanding the essence of change, knowing when to shift, how to shift, and why. It's a conscious evolution, much like how an owl has adapted to thrive in nearly every environment on Earth. Owls are not fast or particularly powerful, but they are masters of adaptation. Over time, they've learned to adjust their hunting methods, their flight patterns, and even their behavior to meet the challenges of diverse habitats.

One day, a young consultant posed a question that lingered with me long after our conversation. She asked, "Why do some companies adapt successfully while others fail?" I explained that the answer is not simply about the speed of change. It lies in the depth of understanding about when to change, how to change, and, most importantly, why to change. This is the essence of adaptation: reading the environment and responding in a way that preserves the company's core while embracing the future.

Understanding Business Ecosystems

In the same way that an owl must understand the dynamics of its environment, the locations of prey, the best hunting times, and the optimal flight routes, businesses must grasp the ecosystems in which they operate. Understanding the business ecosystem is vital, for it shapes how a company can position itself for success in the face of inevitable change.

Every business exists within an ecosystem of sorts. This ecosystem is comprised of not just the company itself but its customers, suppliers, competitors, and even regulators. It also encompasses external factors such as technological shifts, societal trends, and economic forces. The companies that thrive are those that do not view themselves in isolation but as part of a more extensive system that is in constant flux. Over the years, I've worked with companies across a variety of industries, and one truth remains constant: those who understand their ecosystem best are the ones who can adapt successfully.

Consider the case of a family-owned furniture manufacturer I worked with in Michigan. For decades, this company had built its reputation on producing high-quality, handcrafted furniture using traditional methods. But when cheaper imports flooded the market, their business began to struggle. Faced with increasing competition, their initial reaction was to focus on cost-cutting, hoping to compete on price alone. It was a strategy that nearly destroyed them.

However, we took a step back and re-examined their entire business ecosystem. Instead of fixating on the threat of imports, we considered the bigger picture – changing consumer preferences, new distribution channels, and technological advancements. What became clear was that, while mass-market furniture was indeed moving overseas, there was a rising demand for high-end, customizable furniture in urban markets. Professionals with disposable incomes wanted quality craftsmanship but with a modern twist that allowed them to personalize the designs.

We didn't abandon the company's roots; instead, we helped them understand how their deep commitment to craftsmanship could be integrated with the demands of the changing market. The result was a digital platform that allowed customers to customize their pieces online while still preserving the essence of traditional furniture-making techniques. This strategic adaptation not only saved the business but helped it grow, expanding its reach across North America. The company found a way to use its strengths to meet the evolving needs of its ecosystem.

The Three Dimensions of Adaptation

Over the years, through my work with businesses large and small, I have identified three key dimensions of adaptation. Like the owl, which adjusts its hunting techniques, flight patterns, and social behaviors to thrive in various environments, companies must also adapt across multiple dimensions simultaneously. These dimensions—strategic, cultural, and operational—are the pillars upon which successful adaptation rests.

Strategic Adaptation

The first dimension of adaptation is strategic, the most visible, and often the most challenging. It involves changing what a company does and how it does it. This could mean pivoting to a new market, launching new products, or embracing new technologies. But strategic adaptation is more than just a response to external pressures; it is a proactive, thoughtful process of rethinking a company's core value proposition and how it delivers that value to customers.

I once worked with a telecommunications company that had relied heavily on its landline services for decades. However as the world rapidly shifted toward mobile and digital communication, the company's traditional business model was becoming obsolete. The leadership team knew they needed to change, but they weren't sure how. The first step was to help them see that this wasn't just about upgrading technology. It was about understanding how their customers' lives were changing and how they could provide value in the digital age. This required new partnerships, the development of new skills, and a fundamental shift in how the company saw itself. Together, we developed a strategic adaptation framework that helped them identify key areas where change would bring lasting value. The company successfully transitioned from being a provider of phone services to a leader in integrated digital solutions, carving out a new niche in the market.

Cultural Adaptation

The second dimension, and arguably the most difficult, is cultural adaptation. A change in strategy often requires a corresponding shift in organizational culture. This involves changing long-standing behaviors, beliefs, and ways of working, all of which are deeply ingrained in the company's DNA.

One particularly memorable experience was with a Japanese manufacturing company that had decided to expand into Southeast Asia. The leadership believed that success in the region could be achieved by simply transplanting their Japanese operations and culture. However, they quickly ran into resistance. The new employees in Southeast Asia found it difficult to connect with the rigid, hierarchical culture the company had brought with them. There were missed opportunities to innovate and integrate into the local markets, and employee morale suffered.

It became clear that the company needed to embrace a more flexible approach. We worked closely with the leadership team to blend their traditional values with the local customs and work styles. This cultural adaptation allowed the company to expand successfully into Southeast Asia, where they built stronger relationships with local teams and gained a competitive edge. By combining the best of both worlds, the company was able to foster innovation while maintaining its core cultural values.

Operational Adaptation

The third dimension of adaptation is operational. While often overlooked in favor of strategic or cultural changes, operational adaptation is perhaps the most critical. It focuses on how work is done on a day-to-day basis – how processes are structured, how systems function, and how teams collaborate. Without operational adaptation, strategic and cultural changes will falter.

A healthcare provider I worked with faced a similar challenge. They had developed a new strategic vision centered on patient-centric care, but the organization's operations were still siloed and inefficient. The real challenge lies in transforming their operational workflows to support this new model of care. Over several months, we worked with staff across all levels to redesign workflows, streamline processes, and implement new technologies that improved patient coordination. The result was a seamless patient experience and, ultimately, better care outcomes.

Adaptation is not a one-time fix but an ongoing process. As businesses face ever-evolving challenges, they must be prepared to adjust on multiple fronts. The companies that succeed are those that approach adaptation thoughtfully, with an understanding of their ecosystems and a commitment to evolving across strategic, cultural, and operational dimensions.

The Art of Timing

In the complex, fast-paced world of business, the ability to adapt at the right moment is often more valuable than any grand strategy or innovative technology. Adaptation, however, is not just about reacting to circumstances but recognizing the subtle signals in the environment and knowing when to act. The true art of adaptation lies not in rushing to change but in understanding the optimal timing, much like the owl in nature who knows when to adjust its behavior based on the faintest shifts in its surroundings.

Early in my career, I had the opportunity to work with a large retail chain that was committed to staying ahead of the curve, positioning itself as a trendsetter in the marketplace. Their decision to invest heavily in e-commerce in the late 1990s stands as a prime example of how the timing of change can make or break a business. The company was eager to innovate, anticipating the digital revolution that would transform the retail landscape. With the foresight of a company set to become a pioneer, they poured millions into technology that, unfortunately, wasn't quite ready for the market. The problem was not in the technology itself nor the ambition of the company. It was simply too early. Consumers were not yet ready to embrace online shopping as we know it today, and the internet infrastructure at the time was too immature to handle such large-scale changes.

The result was costly. The company, despite its good intentions, found itself nearly bankrupt. Its attempt to leap ahead in a market that wasn't ready for its innovations almost spelled its end. The e-commerce initiative, though visionary, was executed before the necessary technological and cultural conditions were in place. What I learned from this experience is that timing is crucial not just in terms of technology but in understanding market readiness. Being ahead of the curve isn't always an advantage; sometimes, it's about waiting for the right moment to strike.

Years later, I found myself advising a different retailer that faced a similar dilemma. This time, however, we took a more deliberate and measured approach to digital transformation. The lessons of the past were clear. Instead of rushing headlong into adopting every technological trend, we created a staged adaptation plan. This plan not only considered technological readiness but also took into account the critical factor of customer acceptance. We understood that jumping into the future without first aligning the changes with the present state of the market could again lead to failure.

Our plan involved incremental steps that allowed the business to adapt gradually, testing customer reactions along the way and refining the approach as needed. Unlike the earlier experience, where the company's investment was all or nothing, we introduced e-commerce in phases, starting with smaller pilot projects that aligned with the growing comfort of consumers using digital platforms. This strategy allowed the company to build momentum while minimizing the risks of an overly ambitious leap forward.

Understanding Market Readiness

One of the most significant lessons I have learned from both of these experiences is the importance of understanding market readiness. Markets, like individuals, don't change overnight, and they move at different speeds. In my time working with businesses in Southeast Asia, I witnessed firsthand how companies that failed to account for local market conditions wasted resources by trying to implement changes their customers weren't ready for. The business environment in this region, for example, was in many ways different from what I had seen in the United States or Europe, where e-commerce adoption was already gaining traction.

In Southeast Asia, there were markets where the infrastructure simply wasn't in place for online shopping to thrive. Even the simplest logistical issues, such as reliable delivery systems, were barriers that companies failed to understand or address. The lesson here was clear: Success isn't just about pushing out the latest technology or implementing global strategies; it's about recognizing where your market stands and adapting to that reality. Local conditions, cultural nuances, and infrastructural readiness must be part of the equation. The market signals, even those that are subtle, matter significantly in making decisions.

Reading Internal Signals

Just as understanding the external environment is vital, so too is recognizing the internal signals within an organization.

Successful adaptation is as much about an organization's readiness to change as it is about external factors. I recall a recent project with a financial services firm contemplating a broad digital transformation. The company's executives were aware that technology was evolving quickly, but they struggled to gauge how ready their internal teams were to adopt these new tools and processes.

We discovered, however, that change was already beginning in small, grassroots ways. Middle managers, often seen as the most resistant to change, were already experimenting with digital tools and looking for new ways to work more efficiently. These small, unofficial shifts in behavior turned out to be the key to understanding the organization's readiness for broader transformation. The willingness of these employees to experiment with new ways of working indicated that the company wasn't as far from adopting digital tools as the leadership initially thought. This gave us the confidence to push forward with the transformation plan, but only after strengthening and expanding these pockets of innovation within the company.

By recognizing these internal signals, we didn't need to force a top-down shift; instead, we were able to build on the momentum already in place. It was clear that the organization was capable of adapting to change, but it needed time and support to bring all areas of the business in line with the new vision.

Recognizing External Pressure Points

In certain instances, external factors exert such pressure on organizations that adaptation becomes not just a choice but a necessity. The COVID-19 pandemic, for example, forced businesses around the world to rapidly shift to remote work and digital operations. While many companies had been slowly moving toward digitalization, the pandemic accelerated this transformation, making it clear that businesses could no longer delay or ignore the shift.

Fortunately, several clients had already made strides in building adaptive capacity before the pandemic hit. These businesses fared much better during the sudden transition to remote work. They had already invested in digital tools, created flexible work environments, and cultivated a culture that valued adaptation. When the pandemic arrived, they were prepared to pivot swiftly and effectively.

On the other hand, businesses that had neglected these adaptive measures were caught off guard. For them, the rapid shift to digital operations was a significant challenge, requiring major restructuring and significant investment in technology in a very short amount of time. Those who had already built the capacity to adapt were able to weather the storm with much greater ease, reaffirming my belief that preparation is key. Sometimes, external pressure can force change, but those who are ready for it fare far better than those who are not.

Building Adaptive Capacity

Adaptation, I have learned, is not a one-time event; it's a continuous process. Businesses that are successful at adaptation are those that build the capacity to adjust over time, just as an owl can adjust to various changes in its environment. Rather than focusing solely on responding to one specific change or event, successful businesses develop what I call "adaptive muscles." These muscles allow the organization to respond not just to the immediate changes at hand but to ongoing shifts in the market, technology, and customer behavior.

One of the most critical aspects of building adaptive capacity is creating learning systems within an organization. This goes beyond simply gathering data; it's about creating a culture of learning where insights are shared rapidly and used to inform action. In one project with a technology company in California, we worked to establish a system that would allow the company to identify shifts in the market and adjust accordingly. This learning system ensured that the company could continuously monitor changes in the environment and make adjustments when necessary.

At the same time, we encouraged a mindset of experimentation. By framing small, controlled experiments as a way of learning, we reduced the fear of failure and helped teams become more comfortable with trying new approaches. This experimental mindset didn't just lead to better decision-making; it also helped the organization adapt more effectively to changing circumstances.

Finally, building network intelligence was another key aspect of developing adaptive capacity. We encouraged the creation of networks across different departments and levels of the organization to share insights and identify emerging needs for adaptation. These networks acted as a distributed intelligence system that could identify issues before they became problems, creating a more agile organization.

The Human Side of Adaptation
Through all these experiences, I've come to appreciate that adaptation is ultimately a human process. It's not just about

technology, strategy, or systems it's about how people engage with change. One project I recall vividly involved a manufacturing company that was introducing new automation systems. The technical aspects were straightforward, but the human element posed a significant challenge. Experienced workers, many of whom had been with the company for decades, were resistant to the change. They felt that their expertise was being undermined by the new systems, which created a strong pushback against the transition.

Rather than ignoring these concerns or pushing forward with the implementation, we took the time to listen. By engaging these workers in the process and involving them in the design and implementation of the new systems, we discovered that their deep knowledge of the manufacturing process was invaluable. Instead of replacing their expertise, the new systems could be enhanced by their insights. By involving them in the transition, we not only addressed their concerns but turned potential detractors into powerful allies.

Teaching Others to Adapt
In the dynamic world of organizational change, one of the most profound challenges we face as consultants is not merely guiding our clients through transformation but

enabling them to navigate change on their own. While our initial involvement may be critical, the ultimate goal is to empower organizations with the tools and knowledge they need to adapt long after our engagement concludes. This is what I call creating **adaptation capacity** building an organization's internal ability to sense, respond, and thrive amidst change. In this chapter, I will explore how we can achieve this, focusing on strategies like developing frameworks, building skills, and creating support systems that foster a lasting culture of adaptation.

- **Developing Frameworks: A Structured Approach to Change**

Change is inevitable, and organizations must be prepared to respond to it effectively. However, effective adaptation doesn't come from reactive or disjointed actions; it requires a **structured approach** that brings coherence to the process. Over the years, I've learned that organizations thrive when they can respond to change in a thoughtful and deliberate manner. To help organizations become adaptive, we must start by **developing frameworks** that simplify the complex task of responding to change.

When I worked with a large retail bank, one of the first challenges was helping their leadership team understand how adaptation could become a continuous organizational capability. With many teams focused on their immediate tasks, long-term adaptation wasn't a priority. The solution lies in creating a **unified framework** for identifying, evaluating, and responding to shifts in the business environment.

The framework we designed for the bank was simple but powerful. It involved creating clear **processes** for teams to recognize when a change was necessary, how to assess its impact, and how to implement a response. This framework included periodic reviews of external factors like market shifts, technological advancements, and customer behavior patterns. It also outlined clear roles for decision-makers at different levels of the organization to ensure timely and coordinated responses.

The key here is **flexibility**. While frameworks are essential, they must not be so rigid that they hinder creative responses. As organizations evolve, these frameworks must evolve, too. The challenge lies in striking the right balance having enough structure to guide decisions while remaining agile enough to adapt to unforeseen circumstances.

- **Building Skills: Empowering People to Lead Change**

A framework alone won't transform an organization. People must possess the necessary **skills** to recognize the need for adaptation and then act decisively. This involves equipping employees at every level, from senior executives to frontline workers, with both the technical and interpersonal tools needed to drive change.

At the bank, we established **adaptation councils** cross-functional groups of individuals trained in spotting and responding to change. These councils served not only as decision-making bodies but also as **learning hubs** for others across the organization. Through training, mentoring, and hands-on experience, these councils became internal leaders in fostering an adaptive mindset. They didn't just react to change—they anticipated it, often leading their teams to take proactive measures long before a crisis emerged.

To foster a culture of **continuous learning**, adaptation must be seen not as an isolated skill set but as a core competency of all employees. Leaders must be adept at decision-making under uncertainty, and employees must be comfortable navigating ambiguity. This means embedding **soft skills** like communication, influence, and resilience into every level of training. Technical knowledge is critical, but the ability to work collaboratively, manage stress, and persuade others to embrace change is what enables sustainable adaptation.

Over time, this investment in skills pays off. Organizations with a well-developed adaptive skill set are not only better equipped to handle disruptions—they are also more innovative, more engaged, and more capable of leading change within their industries.

- **Creating Support Systems: Reinforcing Change at All Levels**

As organizations begin to implement change, support systems are vital in ensuring that their efforts are sustainable. These systems can take many forms, but their primary function is to provide the infrastructure that reinforces change. In my experience, the most effective support systems integrate **mentoring programs**, **resource networks**, and **feedback loops** that help individuals and teams navigate their adaptation journeys.

Mentoring, for example, plays a crucial role in helping people at different levels of the organization grow and thrive in an adaptive environment. In the case of the bank, we implemented a **mentoring program** where more experienced leaders helped emerging talents navigate the complexities of organizational change. This support allowed leaders to share their **wisdom** while also encouraging mentees to experiment and innovate.

Resource networks are another essential component. Often, people fail to adapt because they lack access to the right information or resources. By establishing systems that provide easy access to knowledge, tools, and expertise, we ensure that teams can respond to change without unnecessary delays or roadblocks.

Lastly, **feedback systems** ensure that adaptation is a continuous process. By regularly collecting feedback from employees, customers, and other stakeholders, organizations can recalibrate their strategies and tactics to stay on track. This not only improves the quality of decision-making but also strengthens the organization's capacity for ongoing adaptation.

- **Measuring Adaptive Success: Going Beyond Traditional Metrics**

One of the most difficult aspects of driving adaptation within organizations is measuring its success. Traditional performance metrics often fail to capture the full impact of adaptive changes, and this can make it challenging for leaders to see the value of their efforts. Over the years, I have developed several strategies to assess adaptive success in ways that go beyond conventional financial metrics.

The first step is to focus on **leading indicators**. These are early signals that adaptation is taking hold. For example, when employees begin to initiate their own improvements or when decision-making speeds up in response to a new challenge, these can be powerful indicators of an adaptive culture. Similarly, when employees demonstrate a willingness to experiment or show comfort with uncertainty, these cultural shifts are important signs of adaptive success.

Another key measure is tracking **cultural changes**. As organizations adapt, their behaviors and attitudes inevitably shift. Employees become more proactive, more resilient, and more open to collaboration. By systematically tracking these cultural measures, we can see how deeply adaptation has become embedded in the organization's fabric. Changes in **employee engagement**, **team cohesion**, and **leadership behaviors** can serve as excellent barometers of adaptive success.

Of course, traditional **performance metrics** are still relevant, but they need to be viewed through the lens of adaptation. Time to market for new initiatives, success rates of pilot programs, and the ability to pivot in response to market conditions are all examples of performance metrics that reflect an organization's adaptive capacity.

- **The Future of Adaptation: Preparing for Tomorrow's Challenges**

As we look toward the future, one thing is certain: the pace of change will only accelerate. Technological advancements, evolving customer expectations, and shifting market dynamics will continue to challenge organizations. In response, organizations must not only be capable of adapting they must **anticipate change** before it happens.

This is where **predictive capabilities** come into play. By leveraging data and analytics, organizations can identify emerging trends, anticipate disruptions, and prepare responses ahead of time. For example, a financial institution could use data-driven insights to predict shifts in consumer behavior or emerging regulatory changes, allowing it to act before these shifts become urgent.

Organizations need to develop more **flexible structures** that can evolve without requiring massive overhauls. Traditional hierarchical designs, where decision-making is centralized, are increasingly inadequate in a world that demands agility. The future of organizational design lies in creating teams and systems that can adjust quickly without the need for structural upheaval.

Innovation networks will become a cornerstone of successful adaptation. As organizations face increasing pressure to innovate, they must connect with external partners, such as start-ups, academic institutions, and other organizations, that can offer new insights and resources. These networks can foster continuous adaptation by introducing fresh perspectives and capabilities that organizations can tap into when needed.

- **The Adaptive Consultant: Modelling Change**

As consultants, we must walk the talk. We can't advise organizations on how to adapt if we aren't willing to model those behaviors ourselves. To be successful, we must continuously update our skills, perspectives, and methodologies. We must be able to work across diverse industries, cultures, and organizational contexts, tailoring our approach to each unique situation. The most successful consultants are those who have mastered the art of **adaptation**. They combine deep expertise with the flexibility to apply it in new, innovative ways.

In my own journey, I have embraced this philosophy, evolving my practices while maintaining the core values and principles that guide my work. Like the owl that hunts by day and by night, we consultants must be able to navigate through diverse conditions. As we help our clients build the capacity for ongoing adaptation, we, too, must be willing to grow, learn, and evolve.

Adaptation as a Continuous Journey

Adaptation isn't just about changing everything; it's about knowing what to preserve and what to modify. It's about balancing stability with flexibility and maintaining core values while evolving practices to meet new challenges. Successful organizations don't just react to change. They actively shape their future by learning to adapt.

As you embark on your consulting journey, remember that the goal is not just to solve today's problems but to help organizations build the capacity to tackle tomorrow's challenges. This is the lasting value we can bring as consultants: the ability to create organizations that can adapt, thrive, and innovate, no matter what the future holds.

PART 2: SILENT STRATEGIST

CHAPTER 3

THE POWER OF QUIET

The boardroom was charged with palpable electricity. Senior executives spoke over one another, their voices rising in intensity with each new interruption. The urgency in their tone, the rapid-fire delivery of words, and the confusion in their expressions made it evident something was wrong. And it was more than just the problem at hand; it was the atmosphere itself, thick with tension.

I sat at the far end of the table, feeling the pressure of being the newest consultant on the project. Every part of me screamed to jump in to offer an analysis, a solution, anything to prove my value to this room of seasoned professionals. There was a temptation to be the voice of reason, the one who could break the deadlock with a clever insight or a quick fix. It was a moment many would describe as a career-defining opportunity. But as the conversation continued to swirl chaotically, I heard the voice of my mentor echo in my mind: "Sometimes, the most powerful thing you can do is stay quiet and truly listen."

I clenched my hands under the table, resisting the urge to speak. I knew that there was wisdom in what my mentor had said. Often, the loudest voices in the room are not the ones that hold the answers. Instead, the most valuable insights come from the quieter spaces, from the pauses in between the noise. That was the first time I truly understood the significance of silence in the consulting world.

It was a moment that would change my approach to consulting forever. By staying silent and not trying to interject, I created a space to listen truly. As the executives continued to argue, I turned my attention to what was happening beyond their words, what they were avoiding saying, and what their actions were betraying. The real issue wasn't the disagreement over the strategy or the market approach. It was the lack of trust, the underlying fear of failure, that no one was willing to address directly. They were all talking about the problem, but none of them were naming it. And that was the crux of the issue.

The Art of Strategic Silence

In many ways, silence can be more potent than words. Nature, in its wisdom, offers numerous examples of how silence can be a tool for survival. Take the owl, for instance. These nocturnal creatures are famous for their silent flight. Their feathers are designed to reduce noise, allowing them to approach their prey undetected. This silence gives them a distinct advantage, enabling them to observe and act without alerting their target.

Similarly, in consulting, knowing when to remain silent is often our greatest strength. Early in my career, I had the privilege of working with a brilliant consultant who seemed to have mastered the art of silence. In meetings with clients, he rarely spoke. But when he did speak, everyone listened. His words carried weight because they were measured, deliberate, and scarce. He wasn't afraid to let silence fill the space, and that gave him an aura of authority. It also gave him the opportunity to hear things others missed.

I once asked him how he managed to maintain such a quiet presence in a room full of talking executives. "Words," he told me, "have more impact when they're rare. Most people are so busy thinking about what they'll say next that they miss what's really happening in the room. If you can be still and observe, the situation will often reveal itself."

This approach served me well during a crisis management project with a technology company that had recently endured several failed product launches. When we were brought in to help, the executives were eager to find someone to blame. They were fixated on the timeline and the market strategy, each person defending their turf and their decisions. Rather than jumping in with suggestions or opinions, our team remained quiet. We listened—really listened.

The results were illuminating. Through active listening and careful observation, we uncovered a pattern that no one had considered: the technical teams were constantly being rushed to meet unrealistic deadlines. No one felt empowered to challenge the aggressive timelines, and as a result, the product launches were consistently premature. By staying silent, we gained an understanding of the dynamics at play, and only then did we begin to formulate our recommendations. The lesson was clear—sometimes, the most valuable insights are found in what isn't being said.

Understanding Active Listening

Active listening is more than just remaining silent. It's about engaging with the moment, observing body language, and picking up on the subtle cues that others may overlook. It's a practice that requires patience and focus. Active listening isn't passive; it demands all your attention. You aren't just hearing words; you are absorbing the atmosphere, the emotions, and the unspoken context that surrounds those words. It's the art of being fully present.

One of my most successful projects began not with a detailed briefing or a list of objectives but with pure listening. I was tasked with helping a family-owned business navigate complex succession challenges. At first glance, the official brief centered around issues of organizational structure and governance. But I quickly realized that there was something deeper at play. By carefully listening during casual conversations in the hallways, observing the dynamics in formal meetings, and even paying attention to what was left unsaid during coffee breaks, I discovered that the true challenge was not structural. It was emotional. The family members were wrestling with the fear that their company's core values might be lost in the process of modernization. These unspoken concerns had not been articulated, but they were central to the decision-making process. By listening, I was able to unearth the underlying fears and develop a more nuanced approach to the succession planning process.

This experience reaffirmed the importance of active listening. It is about taking the time to truly understand the client's world, not just the problems they articulate on paper. It requires stripping away assumptions and judgments and immersing oneself fully in the environment.

The Power of Full Presence

One of the most powerful tools in active listening is the decision to be fully present. In today's world, it's easy to become distracted. Laptops open, phones buzzing, emails piling up. However, during a recent healthcare project, I made a conscious decision to keep my laptop closed during all client interactions. It was a small gesture, but it had a profound impact. By removing the temptation to multitask, I gave my full attention to the conversation at hand. The result was a richer flow of information and more meaningful interactions.

This approach proved particularly effective in a project with a hospital's emergency department. Efficiency metrics indicated that there was room for improvement, but the real insights didn't come from data analysis alone. By quietly observing the staff during their shifts, listening to their frustrations, and watching their workflows firsthand, we discovered that many standard procedures designed to improve efficiency actually slowed down patient care. It wasn't the guidelines that were at fault; it was the way they were being implemented. Through active listening and a commitment to full presence, we identified the real bottlenecks and re-engineered the workflow, which led to improved patient outcomes and a more efficient department.

Emotional Awareness in Listening

Listening is not just about hearing words. It's also about understanding the emotions that those words convey. People often communicate more through their tone, body language, and facial expressions than through the words themselves. Being aware of these emotional cues is critical for consultants, as they provide a much deeper understanding of a situation than surface-level communication alone.

During a retail transformation project, I was struck by how the tone of voice and body language of store managers contradicted the words they were saying. On the surface, they seemed to agree with the proposed changes to store operations, but their body language told a different story.

They seemed disengaged, frustrated, and resistant. It was clear that they felt their expertise and the pride they took in their store operations were being overlooked.

Recognizing this emotional undercurrent allowed us to address the issue more effectively. Previous consultants had implemented changes without considering the emotional attachment these managers had to their work. By acknowledging and respecting those emotions, we were able to co-create solutions that honored the managers' sense of ownership while still modernizing the operations. This emotional awareness made the difference between a successful transformation and one that would have been met with resistance and resentment.

The Science of Listening

Effective communication is the cornerstone of successful consultancy. As consultants, we often find ourselves in rooms filled with stakeholders, each with their own opinions, emotions, and priorities. It is not uncommon to leave these meetings with only a fraction of the information truly absorbed. In fact, research suggests that we typically remember only 25 to 50% of what we hear. This is not an acceptable rate of information retention for anyone, let alone for those of us who depend on clear, precise, and insightful communication to guide decision-making. Through years of experience, I've developed a systematic approach to listening, a way of capturing the full spectrum of what's being said, both in words and in silence.

Mental Preparation

Every impactful interaction begins long before the conversation itself. The mind is a powerful tool, but it is also easily distracted. To listen effectively, one must first clear away the clutter of thoughts and preconceived notions. This process of mental preparation is not merely a fleeting moment of focus; it is a commitment to be present and open to what the conversation will reveal.

Before any significant client interaction, I make a point of arriving early. It's a ritual that allows me to take a few quiet moments to center myself and detach from the rest of the day's demands. Sometimes, this means sitting in my car before entering the building or finding a corner in the client's office to breathe deeply and clear my mind. The goal is simple: to prepare myself to listen without bias or preconceived ideas and to allow the conversation to unfold without filtering it through prior expectations.

I recall a high-stakes merger negotiation where the stakes were high, the emotions intense, and the complexities far-reaching. The day before each meeting, I would spend fifteen minutes in silence, allowing my mind to settle. This time was invaluable it helped me become attuned to shifts in tone, body language, and subtle changes in the dynamics of the conversation. I could detect nuances that others might have missed, such as a slight change in a stakeholder's facial expression or an unexpected pause in the dialogue. These small moments often provided me with the insight needed to navigate the next phase of negotiations effectively.

Physical Awareness

Our physical state is inextricably linked to our mental capacity for listening. How we feel, how much rest we've had, and even the environment in which we work all affect our ability to absorb and process information. As a consultant, it became clear to me that the way I managed my physical state directly influenced my effectiveness in listening.

I learned this lesson the hard way during a particularly demanding project in Singapore. I had flown across several time zones and was dealing with jet lag, compounded by back-to-back meetings that left me physically drained.

Despite my best efforts to stay engaged, I found myself struggling to stay focused during critical conversations. In one instance, a senior executive was detailing the future direction of the company, and I realized only after the meeting that I had missed key pieces of the conversation due to sheer exhaustion.

This experience led me to rethink how I manage my physical state before and during meetings. Now, I take deliberate steps to ensure I am physically prepared to listen. This might involve scheduling short walks between meetings, engaging in breathing exercises to maintain my energy levels, or even standing during longer sessions to avoid the lethargy that comes from sitting for extended periods. When I am physically alert, my capacity for listening improves dramatically, and I can catch the nuances in a conversation that might otherwise pass unnoticed.

Documentation Techniques

The act of listening is inextricably tied to the ability to record and document key insights without allowing note-taking to become a distraction. While traditional note-taking can be helpful, it often pulls attention away from the conversation itself. This is a critical pitfall for consultants who need to remain engaged while simultaneously capturing important details.

Over the years, I've developed a streamlined system for documentation that allows me to keep my focus on the speaker while recording essential points. I use quick notations, short phrases, or keywords that capture the essence of the conversation without overwhelming my cognitive resources. This approach enables me to maintain eye contact and stay engaged while ensuring that nothing important is lost.

An example of this method was when I worked with a pharmaceutical company. The complexity of the discussions required me to map conversations in real time. I didn't just note down what was being said; I paid attention to the energy, emotion, and non-verbal cues accompanying the words. By doing so, I was able to identify patterns and hidden issues that a standard meeting summary would have missed. This deeper layer of insight allowed the team to make informed decisions that improved their market positioning.

The Power of Strategic Questions

Listening does not end with simply hearing words; it also involves creating opportunities for insight by asking the right questions at the right time. Strategic questions can transform a conversation from a simple exchange of information into a powerful tool for discovery. The ability to ask the right question at the right moment can unlock insights that would otherwise remain hidden.

During a strategy project with a technology start-up, we faced the challenge of identifying new growth opportunities. Rather than offering immediate solutions to their growth challenges, I asked the founding team, "If you could start over today, knowing what you know now, what would you do differently?" The room fell into a deep silence. The question had struck a chord, and for nearly five minutes, no one spoke. In that stillness, however, the team uncovered critical insights about their market positioning and growth trajectory. The answers that followed were far more transformative than any quick fix I could have provided.

Types of Questions

Over time, I've learned to use different types of questions to serve distinct purposes. Each type of question plays a specific role in guiding the conversation and uncovering new perspectives.

- **Clarifying Questions**: These are essential for ensuring that I fully understand the speaker's message and show respect for their expertise. For example, when working with a manufacturing client, I often ask, "Could you help me understand how this process worked before the recent changes?" This question was simple yet effective, as it revealed critical context about why certain changes were meeting resistance and helped me better understand the challenges they were facing.

- **Perspective-Shifting Questions**: These questions are designed to help people view their situation from a new angle. During a change management project, I asked a team, "How would your most satisfied customer describe this service?" This question prompted the team to reflect on the strengths of their service offering, many of which they had taken for granted. It reshaped their approach to customer satisfaction and service improvement.

- **Future-Focused Questions**: These questions guide conversations from problem analysis to solution finding. When a retail client was struggling to adapt to online competition, I asked, "What would wild success look like three years from now?" This question shifted their focus from defensive tactics to innovative strategies, helping them chart a course for long-term growth.

Creating Space for Silence

In today's fast-paced business environment, silence is often seen as uncomfortable or unproductive. However, silence can be a powerful tool for reflection, deeper understanding, and innovative thinking. One of the key lessons I've learned throughout my career is the importance of building intentional spaces for silence in consulting projects.

Building Quiet into Projects

I now make it a point to incorporate "listening phases" into every project I manage. These are deliberate periods of quiet observation and reflection that allow both the client and the consultant to process information without interruption. These silent periods often yield insights that can't be captured through traditional methods.

For example, at a manufacturing client, we scheduled regular intervals during which our consulting team would simply observe operations. We didn't ask questions or make suggestions; we just watched. These silent observation periods revealed workflow issues that we hadn't anticipated and allowed us to provide more targeted, impactful recommendations.

Reflection Sessions

In addition to silent observation, I have found that incorporating "quiet hours" into workshops can have a profound impact on the quality of subsequent discussions. When working with a financial services client, we designated a portion of our workshop days as "quiet time." During this period, participants were encouraged to process the information and insights they had gathered without engaging in active discussion. The impact on the quality of the conversations that followed was remarkable. Ideas flowed more freely, and the insights generated during the reflective periods were far more profound.

Digital Silence

Another powerful method for creating space for reflection is digital silence. In many critical client meetings, I turn off all devices and encourage others to do the same. In a world constantly bombarded by notifications, creating this space for focused listening has led to deeper, more meaningful conversations. The simple act of disconnecting from technology allows everyone in the room to be fully present and engaged, enhancing the quality of the interaction.

The Challenge of Silence

Maintaining silence in the world of consulting is an often-overlooked skill one that doesn't come easily, especially for those of us who have been trained to fill every moment with words. As consultants, we are conditioned to provide quick answers to offer solutions and advice at the drop of a hat. Yet, in my early career, I began to realize that silence, though uncomfortable, held immense value in uncovering deeper truths, understanding clients more profoundly, and arriving at the most effective solutions.

The first time I truly understood the power of silence was during a project with a troubled technology company. The company had been facing significant challenges in meeting its targets, and there was palpable tension in the room as the leadership team gathered to discuss their struggles. As I sat across from them, I felt the pressure to speak up, to offer an immediate solution to resolve their issues. I wanted to dive in, direct the conversation, and propose strategies that might ease their anxiety. But something inside me urged restraint.

I decided to try something different. Rather than jumping straight into problem-solving mode, I chose to ask about their greatest concerns about the issues they felt were at the core of the company's struggles, and then I stayed quiet. I resisted the urge to fill the silence with words. The room grew heavy with stillness, and the discomfort was palpable. I could see people shifting in their seats, glancing nervously at one another, unsure of how to respond. For a long moment, the only sound in the room was the faint hum of the air conditioning.

As the silence stretched on, something remarkable happened. One of the senior leaders finally spoke, admitting that the targets had been set unrealistically high. Another leader confessed that the resources allocated to the project had been woefully insufficient. These were insights that might have remained hidden had I not given the space for them to emerge. The silence, though uncomfortable at first, became a powerful tool for revealing the deeper issues that were hindering their progress.

Learning to Be Comfortable with Silence

This experience marked a turning point in my approach to consulting. I began to see silence not as a void to be filled but as a fertile space for deeper understanding and reflection. But learning to be comfortable with silence didn't happen overnight. It took deliberate practice and a shift in mindset.

Personal Development was the first area in which I focused my efforts. I began incorporating meditation and mindfulness practices into my daily routine. These practices helped me become more comfortable with quiet moments, not just in the professional setting but in my personal life as well. Over time, I learned to quiet my mind and resist the impulse to speak in every pause or lull in conversation. This mental discipline significantly improved my ability to listen deeply, not only to what was being said but also to what was being left unsaid.

In parallel, I began to introduce these principles to the teams I led. **Team Training** became an essential part of project preparation. I implemented exercises in silent observation and active listening, where team members were encouraged to observe without speaking to listen attentively without interruption. These exercises helped my team develop a better understanding of clients' needs, priorities, and challenges. More importantly, they taught us to be present in the moment, to allow the conversation to unfold naturally, and to resist the temptation to offer solutions prematurely.

Working with **clients** on the concept of silence was another challenge. Many clients initially found the practice of maintaining quiet uncomfortable. In cultures that value action and quick decision-making, silence often feels like a stall or an inability to make progress. Over time, I learned to explain the value of these quiet moments upfront, framing them not as a lack of action but as an essential tool for deeper understanding. I found that when clients understood the purpose of silence, they were more willing to embrace it as a tool for productive dialogue.

Listening Across Cultures

Consulting in a global context added another layer of complexity to the challenge of silence. I quickly learned that the way silence is perceived and used varies greatly across cultures. As I worked with clients from different parts of the world, I discovered that listening takes many different forms, and silence itself carries distinct meanings depending on the cultural context.

One of my earliest lessons came during a project in Japan. There, I was introduced to the concept of **"nemawashi,"** a practice of informal, quiet consensus-building that happens before formal decisions are made. This process, though silent, was crucial in ensuring that all stakeholders were aligned before any public discussions or decisions took place. The value placed on non-verbal communication and the unspoken understanding that is built during these quiet moments was an eye-opener.

In **Asian cultures**, where indirect communication is often preferred, silence can convey far more than words. During a project in China, I learned that silence could indicate disagreement rather than agreement. This was a stark contrast to Western business norms, where silence might be interpreted as agreement or a lack of participation. Understanding these nuances allowed me to navigate complex negotiations better and avoid misunderstandings.

In the **Middle East**, I discovered that silence often serves a different purpose altogether. Relationship-building conversations, which might seem tangential in Western business settings, are of utmost importance in the Middle East. Here, silence is not about discomfort or hesitation; rather, it is an acknowledgment of the personal and emotional connections that form the foundation of business decisions. Learning to listen to personal stories and understanding the role of relationship-building in decision-making processes proved to be just as important as analyzing business data.

The Impact of Technology

In today's hyper-connected world, where technology dominates every aspect of life, maintaining silence can be a formidable challenge. Virtual meetings, constant emails, and the constant pinging of notifications can make it nearly impossible to find moments of stillness and reflection. During the global pandemic, when remote work became the norm, I had to develop new approaches to create quiet spaces in virtual environments.

We implemented **"digital quiet rooms"** during virtual meetings places where team members could reflect without interruption, even when working remotely. This was especially important when conducting sensitive discussions or brainstorming sessions that required deep thought and focus. Additionally, we modified our communication protocols, establishing clear guidelines about device usage and creating structured spaces for reflection. These efforts were crucial in helping teams maintain a sense of focus, even in the midst of constant digital distractions.

In the realm of **documentation**, we also adopted. Virtual meetings can make it easy to miss subtle nonverbal cues, so we developed new methods for capturing and sharing these cues. This included encouraging participants to use video and visual aids more intentionally, as well as implementing post-meeting debriefs where we would review not only the spoken content of the meeting but also the unspoken signals that may have been missed.

Teaching the Power of Quiet

As I continued to refine my approach, I began to recognize the responsibility we, as consultants, have in helping our clients develop better listening skills. Many organizations are action-oriented and focused on rapid problem-solving, often at the expense of truly listening to their employees or customers. My work with a fast-growing technology company was a perfect example of how powerful silence can be in fostering innovation.

We introduced regular **"listening sessions,"** where senior leaders practiced staying quiet and actively listening to their team members. These sessions were initially met with resistance, but the results were transformative. As leaders learned to listen without interrupting, employees felt more valued and engaged. This shift in communication fostered a greater sense of collaboration and led to more innovative ideas being brought to the table.

In other organizations, we helped create **listening cultures** from the top down. Working with a retail chain, we assisted executives in modeling effective listening behaviors. The impact on communication was profound. When leadership demonstrated the value of listening, employees at all levels followed suit, creating an environment where ideas flowed more freely, and collaboration became the norm.

For a healthcare provider, we designed physical and virtual spaces specifically for quiet reflection and active listening. These spaces became sanctuaries where individuals could step away from the noise of their busy workdays and engage in focused, meaningful conversations. The result was an organization that communicated more effectively, with a renewed focus on patient care and staff well-being.

The Silent Advantage

In the world of consulting, as in nature, the ability to maintain strategic silence can often determine success. Like the owl's silent flight, our quiet presence allows us to gather crucial information and strike at the right moment with meaningful insights. Silence is not about being passive; it is about creating the space for deeper understanding and more effective action.

As you continue to develop your consulting practice, remember that sometimes, the most powerful thing you can do is simply listen. In the fast-paced, noise-filled world of modern business, the ability to pause, listen, and allow space for reflection is a rare and valuable skill. Master this skill, and you'll find yourself noticing opportunities and insights that others miss entirely.

CHAPTER 4
PRECISION & FOCUS

The clock showed 3 AM as I stared at a wall of data in my client's office. Somewhere in these numbers lay the key to solving their profitability crisis, but after sixteen hours of analysis, everything was starting to blur. Then I remembered watching a documentary about how owls hunt, their remarkable ability to focus on a single target among countless distractions, maintaining unwavering attention until the perfect moment to strike. That memory changed my approach entirely.

The Art of Precision in Consulting

In my fifteen years as a management consultant, I've learned that precision isn't just about being accurate; it's about knowing exactly where to focus your attention and energy. Like an owl zeroing in on its prey among the rustling leaves, a skilled consultant must identify the critical factors that will drive success amid the noise of business complexity.

One of my earliest projects taught me this lesson the hard way. Working with a struggling retail chain, our team gathered mountains of data about everything from store layouts to staff schedules. We produced beautiful analyses and comprehensive reports, but we weren't improving our performance. It wasn't until we narrowed our focus to three critical metrics that we started seeing real improvements.

The Three Elements of Consulting Precision

Through years of experience across industries, I've identified three fundamental elements that determine a consultant's ability to work with precision:

Strategic Focus: The first project I led independently was nearly derailed by a lack of strategic focus. The client, a mid-sized manufacturer, wanted to improve their operations. We began analyzing every aspect of their business supply chain, production, sales, and human resources. While this comprehensive approach seemed thorough, it actually prevented us from making meaningful progress.

The turning point came when we narrowed our focus to their core manufacturing processes. By concentrating our efforts on this critical area, we achieved more in two weeks than we had in the previous two months. This experience taught me that precision often means choosing what not to do.

Years later, working with a telecommunications company, I applied this lesson from day one. Instead of trying to address all their challenges simultaneously, we identified their customer churn rate as the single most important factor affecting their profitability. This focused approach led to a 23% reduction in customer churn within six months.

Analytical Rigor: Precision in consulting requires more than just focusing on the right issues. It demands excellence in how we analyze and solve problems. During a project with a pharmaceutical company, we needed to optimize their research and development portfolio. The amount of data was overwhelming, but success depended on our ability to maintain analytical precision despite the complexity.

We developed a systematic approach to handling complex data sets:

- **Data Validation:** Before diving into analysis, we established rigorous protocols for verifying data accuracy. This meant cross-referencing multiple sources, questioning assumptions, and documenting our validation process.
- **Pattern Recognition:** We looked for recurring patterns and relationships in the data, always asking ourselves

what these patterns meant for the business. This helped us move from raw data to actionable insights.

- **Impact Assessment:** For every finding, we calculated the potential impact on the business. This helped us prioritize our recommendations and focus on changes that would make the most difference.

- **Execution Excellence:** The third element of precision is excellence in execution. I learned this lesson while working with a retail bank implementing a new customer service strategy. Our analysis was perfect, and our recommendations were solid, but our initial implementation was too broad and unfocused.

We regrouped and developed what I call the "precision implementation approach":

- **Clear Prioritization:** Instead of trying to implement everything at once, we identified the three changes that would have the biggest impact and focused on those first.

- **Detailed Planning:** For each change, we created detailed implementation plans that specified exactly what needed to happen, who would do it, and when it would be done.

- **Regular Monitoring:** We established clear metrics for success and monitored them weekly, allowing us to make quick adjustments when needed.

The Psychology of Precision

One aspect of precision that often gets overlooked is the psychological component. Like an owl maintaining complete focus despite distractions, consultants must develop mental discipline to work with precision.

Working with a technology startup, I noticed how easily team members got distracted by new ideas and opportunities. While creativity is valuable, lack of focus was preventing them from executing effectively on any single initiative.

We implemented what I call "precision thinking protocols":

Mental Preparation Before major analytical tasks or client meetings, we take time to clear our minds and focus our attention. This might mean a brief meditation, a quiet walk, or simply a few minutes of focused breathing.

Distraction Management We identified common distractions and developed strategies to manage them. This included turning off phone notifications during analysis sessions and scheduling specific times for email checking.

Energy Management We recognized that mental precision requires physical energy, so we started paying attention to sleep, exercise, and nutrition during intensive project phases.

Tools for Precision

Over the years, I've developed and refined various tools to help maintain precision in consulting work. These aren't just analytical frameworks they're practical approaches to maintaining focus and accuracy under pressure.

The Precision Matrix During a complex transformation project with a financial services firm, I developed what I call the Precision Matrix. This tool helps consultants maintain focus on what matters most:

- Impact Assessment We rate potential initiatives based on their likely impact on key business metrics.
- Implementation Difficulty We evaluate how challenging each initiative will be to implement successfully.
- Resource Requirements We assess the people, time, and money needed for each initiative.

- This matrix helped us identify "precision targets" initiatives with high-impact potential and manageable implementation challenges.
- The Focus Funnel Another tool I've found valuable is the Focus Funnel, which helps filter out distractions and maintain precision in analysis and recommendation development:
- **Strategic Alignment:** Does this align with the core project objectives?
- **Impact Potential**: What's the potential return on investment?
- **Implementation Feasibility:** Can this be implemented effectively with available resources?

Only initiatives that pass through all levels of the funnel receive detailed attention and resources.

Precision in Communication

Precision isn't just about analysis. It's equally important in how we communicate with clients. Early in my career, I made the mistake of trying to share everything I knew about a topic. Now I understand that precision in communication means sharing exactly what the client needs to know, no more and no less.

During a recent strategy project, instead of presenting our entire analysis, we focused on three key insights and their implications. This focused approach led to better understanding and faster decision-making by the client team.

- **Written Communication:** In written communications, precision means:
- **Clear Structure:** Every document should have a clear purpose and logical flow.
- **Concise Expression:** Using exactly the words needed to convey meaning, no more and no less.
- **Actionable Content:** Ensuring every piece of information leads to clear next steps.
- Verbal Communication: In meetings and presentations, precision requires:
- **Focused Messages:** Delivering key points without unnecessary detail.
- **Targeted Examples:** Use specific examples that directly support the main points.
- **Clear Recommendations:** Make sure action items and next steps are clearly understood.

The Role of Experience in Precision

Experience plays a crucial role in developing precision in consulting. Like an owl that becomes more efficient with each hunt, consultants develop better judgment about where to focus their attention.

Early in my career, I often got lost in details that ultimately proved irrelevant. Now, I can more quickly identify the critical factors that will determine project success. This isn't about cutting corners; it's about knowing where precision matters most.

- **Building Experience:** For newer consultants, I recommend:
- **Careful Documentation:** Keep records of what worked and what didn't in different situations.
- **Pattern Recognition:** Look for similarities and differences across projects and industries.

Mentor Relationships Learn from experienced consultants about how they maintain precision in their work.

Teaching Precision

As a senior consultant, part of my role is teaching others how to work with precision. This involves helping them understand:

- **When to Dive Deep:** Not every issue requires the same level of precision. Teaching others when to dig deeper and when to maintain a higher-level view is crucial.
- **How to Maintain Focus:** Helping team members develop their techniques for maintaining focus and precision under pressure.
- **The Importance of Balance:** Understanding that precision doesn't mean perfection – it means being exactly as detailed as the situation requires.

Technology and Precision

Modern technology offers new tools for maintaining precision in consulting work, but it also presents new challenges. During a recent digital transformation project, we found that data analytics tools both helped and hindered our precision efforts.

The key is using technology to enhance rather than replace human judgment:

- **Data Analytics:** Using advanced analytics to identify patterns and relationships that might not be visible otherwise.
- **Project Management Tools**: Employing software to help maintain precision in planning and execution.
- **Communication Platforms:** Utilizing technology to enable precise communication across global teams.

As business environments become more complex and fast-paced, the ability to maintain precision will become even more crucial. Future consultants will need to:

- **Develop New Skills:** Building capabilities in areas like data science while maintaining traditional consulting precision.
- **Adapt to New Tools:** Learning to use new technologies while maintaining focus on what matters most.
- **Balance Speed and Accuracy:** Finding ways to maintain precision while working at the increasingly fast pace that modern business demands.

The Precision Imperative

Like the owl's precise strike, successful consulting requires a combination of focus, timing, and execution excellence. The ability to maintain precision under pressure isn't just a skill. It's a competitive advantage in today's complex business environment.

Precision isn't about perfectionism. It's about focusing your energy and attention where they'll have the greatest impact. As you develop your consulting career, work on building your capacity for precision while maintaining the flexibility to adapt to changing circumstances.

The next time you feel overwhelmed by the complexity of a consulting engagement, remember the owl, which is focused, precise, and effective. With practice and dedication, you, too, can develop the precision that marks truly exceptional consultants.

Delivering Actionable Solutions

The moment remains vivid in my memory. I stood before a room of executives who had just invested three months and significant resources in our consulting engagement. My team produced a comprehensive 200-page report filled with data, analysis, and recommendations. As I finished the presentation, the CEO looked at me and asked a simple question that would forever change my approach to consulting: "So what exactly do you want us to do on Monday morning?"

That question crystallized one of the most important lessons in consulting: the gap between insight and action is where many consulting projects fail. Just as an owl's keen vision would be useless without its ability to strike precisely, our sharpest insights mean nothing if clients can't turn them into action.

Through fifteen years of consulting experience, I've learned that creating truly actionable solutions requires a deep understanding of three fundamental elements: clarity, feasibility, and ownership. A project with a major automotive supplier taught me this lesson in stark terms.

The company was struggling with supply chain inefficiencies. Our initial analysis was thorough, identifying numerous improvement opportunities. However, when implementation began, we discovered that our recommendations, while technically sound, weren't gaining traction. The reason? We hadn't considered the practical constraints of their operation.

After this experience, I developed what I call the "Monday Morning Test." If a solution can't be started immediately and shows progress within the first week, it needs to be refined. This approach has transformed how I develop recommendations.

Understanding Organizational Reality

One of my most humbling experiences came early in my career. Working with a retail bank, I developed what I thought was a brilliant reorganization plan. The analysis was solid, the numbers added up, and the logic was impeccable. Yet six months later, barely 20% of the recommendations had been implemented.

The missing piece was an understanding of the organization's reality, its culture, capabilities, and constraints. Since then, I've learned to spend significant time understanding these elements before developing solutions:

Organizational Culture During a recent project with a technology company, we realized that their entrepreneurial culture would reject any solution that felt too structured or bureaucratic. Instead of our standard approach, we created a framework that emphasized experimentation and rapid iteration, which aligned with their cultural preferences.

This meant breaking down our recommendations into small, testable hypotheses that teams could validate quickly. The result was much higher adoption and faster results than our traditional approach would have achieved.

Capability Assessment Working with a manufacturing client, we discovered that their technical capabilities were significantly different across locations. A solution that worked perfectly in their main plant would have failed in their smaller facilities. This led us to develop tiered implementation plans that matched each location's capabilities.

We created a capability matrix that helped us understand what each facility could realistically achieve in different timeframes. This allowed us to sequence our recommendations in a way that built capabilities progressively rather than overwhelming teams with changes they weren't ready to handle.

Resource Constraints: A healthcare provider taught me the importance of intimately understanding resource limitations. While our initial recommendations were theoretically sound, they required more staff training time than was practically available. We had to redesign our solutions to work within their actual constraints rather than assumed ideals.

The Architecture of Actionable Solutions

Over time, I've developed a framework for creating solutions that bridge the gap between theory and practice. This framework emerged from both successes and failures across dozens of projects.

Clear Prioritization: Working with a telecommunications company, we faced a common consulting challenge with too many good ideas. The client could have pursued any of twenty different initiatives, all with positive ROI. The key was helping them understand which ones to do first.

We developed a prioritization framework that went beyond simple metrics like ROI or ease of implementation. It included factors such as:

- **Sequential Dependencies:** Understanding which initiatives needed to happen first to enable others.
- **Resource Competition Identifying:** which projects would compete for the same scarce resources.
- **Organizational Energy:** Assessing how much change the organization could absorb at once.

This framework helped the client focus on the five initiatives that would create the most value while building momentum for future changes.

Practical Implementation Plans: A consumer goods company taught me the importance of detailed implementation planning. Their previous consulting engagements had produced impressive strategies that failed in execution. Working with their teams, we developed what I call "granular implementation plans."

These plans broke down each recommendation into specific actions, each with:

Clear Ownership Identifying not just departments but specific individuals responsible for each action.

- **Resource Requirements:** Detailing exactly what people, time, and money would be needed.
- **Success Metrics:** Establishing clear, measurable indicators of progress and success.
- **Timeline and Milestones:** Creating a realistic schedule with clear checkpoints for monitoring progress.

The Power of Progressive Implementation

One of my most successful projects involved transforming a financial services company's operations completely. Instead of trying to change everything at once, we developed a progressive implementation approach that built momentum through early wins.

- Phase Zero: Quick Wins We identified changes that could be implemented immediately with existing resources. These early successes-built credibility and enthusiasm for the larger transformation.
- Foundation Building: We focused on developing key capabilities and systems that would enable more complex changes later.
- Scaling and Integration: Only after establishing a solid foundation did we begin implementing more ambitious changes.

Creating Ownership Through Collaboration

A crucial lesson I've learned is that solutions imposed by consultants rarely stick. True change requires genuine ownership by the client organization. During a project with a retail chain, we transformed our approach from presenting solutions to co-creating them with the client team.

Collaborative Design Instead of developing recommendations in isolation, we created working sessions where client teams actively participated in solution development. This meant:

- **Joint Problem Definition:** Working with client teams to ensure we understood the real issues, not just the symptoms.
- **Solution Workshops:** Regular sessions where consultants and client teams worked together to develop and refine solutions.
- **Implementation Planning:** Involving key stakeholders in creating detailed implementation plans.

Technology Integration in Solution Design

Modern consulting requires a deep understanding of how technology can either facilitate or impede the successful implementation of a solution. It's not enough to simply design an ideal system or strategy on paper; the real challenge lies in bridging the gap between vision and execution. In today's fast-paced and ever-evolving business landscape, technology's role in consulting cannot be underestimated. Technology offers new opportunities, but it also brings with it significant complexities. During a recent digital transformation project, we found that the key to success is balancing technological possibilities with the practical limitations that come with any system implementation. The ability to integrate new technology into an organization's existing infrastructure is no longer just a technical concern; it is a crucial strategic consideration for the entire consulting process.

- **Current Systems: Understanding Existing Technology Infrastructure**

The first step in designing any technological solution is to fully understand the current systems that an organization has in place. Often, clients will want to implement cutting-edge solutions without giving adequate thought to how those solutions will mesh with their existing infrastructure. This can be a costly mistake. Without a comprehensive understanding of the current systems, the implementation process runs the risk of failing to meet expectations, not because the solution itself is flawed but because it does not align with or integrate well into the environment it is meant to enhance.

For instance, during a recent project for an insurance company, we encountered significant hurdles when we attempted to integrate new cloud-based tools into their legacy systems. The insurance firm had a robust IT infrastructure that had served them well for years, but the company's internal processes were built around outdated software platforms. While the cloud solution offered new capabilities, its success relied on a seamless connection with the older systems. We quickly realized that without a detailed mapping of both the old and new technologies, we would have faced costly setbacks.

The key to avoiding such challenges is a thorough assessment of the existing technology. By understanding the architecture, capacity, and limitations of current systems, consultants can plan for potential integration issues. This also involves understanding how data flows through the organization, what systems are critical to day-to-day operations, and identifying any technical debt that could slow down the implementation of new solutions.

- **User Capabilities: Assessing Technical Skills and Readiness**

While technology itself is often the focal point of solution design, it is crucial to remember that people are the ones who will ultimately use and maintain these systems. For any solution to be effective, the users, whether they are employees, customers, or partners, must possess the technical skills to interact with the system in the way that was intended. Consultants often make the mistake of focusing too much on the technical specifications of a system, forgetting to account for the end users' capabilities.

In one case, we were brought in to assist with the rollout of a customer relationship management (CRM) system for a retail client. While the system was state-of-the-art and capable of automating numerous processes, the company's workforce had limited experience with such advanced software. As a result, initial implementation efforts were met with resistance, confusion, and frustration. Employees struggled to understand the user interface, which led to a decline in adoption rates.

To avoid such outcomes, it is essential to assess the technical capabilities of the people who will interact with the new system. This goes beyond merely gauging their familiarity with similar systems; it also involves understanding their comfort level with technology and identifying any training needs. During the initial stages of any project, consultants must work closely with client stakeholders to identify the gaps in user knowledge and develop targeted training programs that will help bridge those gaps.

- **Change Management Requirements: Planning for Adoption and Sustainability**

A successful technology integration is not just about implementing a new system. It's about ensuring that the system is adopted and used consistently over time. This is where change management becomes a critical component. The best-designed system will fail if it does not receive the buy-in from the people who are expected to use it. In many cases, the introduction of new technology triggers a sense of anxiety and resistance among employees, who may feel that the new system will disrupt their workflow or render their skills obsolete.

During a project with a financial services provider, we learned just how essential it is to factor in the human element of technology adoption. Our team had developed a sophisticated data analytics tool to help the client make better business decisions. However, without a comprehensive change management strategy, the project ran into significant challenges. Some employees were concerned that the new tool would make their roles redundant, while others were skeptical about its usefulness.

To manage this resistance and ensure that the technology was successfully adopted, we implemented a multi-phase change management strategy. This strategy included clear communication about the system's benefits, a series of hands-on training sessions, and the creation of support teams to assist employees throughout the transition.

Consultants must recognize that successful technology integration requires a holistic approach that incorporates both the technical and human aspects of implementation. By planning for change management and ensuring that the system is aligned with the organization's culture and employee capabilities, the likelihood of sustained success increases significantly.

Measuring Success and Adjusting Course

The implementation of a new system should never be viewed as a one-time event. Technology integration is an ongoing process that requires continuous monitoring, feedback, and adjustments. A key element of our consulting approach is the creation of a framework to monitor the success of the implementation, both during and after the rollout. This framework includes a mix of leading and lagging indicators that provide a comprehensive picture of the system's effectiveness.

In one notable case, we worked with a healthcare provider to integrate an electronic medical records (EMR) system. The system was designed to streamline patient data management and improve overall efficiency. However, initial feedback indicated that the system was not being used to its full potential, with many staff members still relying on paper-based methods.

To measure success, we used a variety of key performance indicators (KPIs), including user adoption rates, system uptime, and patient satisfaction metrics. We also held regular review meetings with stakeholders to assess how well the system was meeting their needs and whether there were any emerging issues. As we monitored the system, we identified several issues, including a lack of adequate user training and gaps in integration with other systems.

PART 3: COLLABORATION & LEADERSHIP

CHAPTER 5

TEAMWORK IN OWL COLONIES

It was past midnight in Singapore, and our consulting team sat in a dimly lit conference room, facing a crisis that would require every ounce of our collective skill. The client, a major telecommunications company, had thrown us an urgent challenge a need for a complete strategic overhaul by the next morning. My colleagues were visibly exhausted, having worked tirelessly through the night, but we were determined to find a solution.

As I gazed around the room at the tired faces of my team, I couldn't help but be reminded of something I had learned years earlier about barn owls. These creatures, often misunderstood as solitary hunters, actually thrive in loose colonies. Despite their tendency to hunt alone, they often share crucial information about hunting grounds and collaborate in raising their young. This behavior, where individuals contribute to the group's collective success without necessarily sacrificing their independence, mirrored the dynamic we needed to develop as a team.

This observation sparked an epiphany. The very essence of owl colonies of loosely-knit groups that share information and work in harmony could offer a new framework for how we could approach our crisis. As we scrambled to organize a new strategy on the fly, I realized that our success depended not on individual brilliance but on our ability to collaborate efficiently, leveraging each team member's unique skills and perspectives.

The Power of Collective Wisdom

In the twelve years I spent in consulting, I had come to understand that teamwork is a delicate yet crucial element of any successful project. More often than not, it's not the technical expertise or even the grand ideas that drive success; it's the ability of a team to work cohesively. Much like owl colonies that thrive on mutual support and shared knowledge, effective consulting teams are built on the collective wisdom of their members.

I think back to an early experience in my career, a defining moment that shaped my approach to team dynamics. Our team had been tasked with managing the merger of two large manufacturing companies. The senior partner assigned to the project was widely regarded as a genius, known for his sharp intellect and ability to solve complex problems single-handedly. But as the merger unfolded, it became abundantly clear that his brilliance, while impressive, could not overcome the scale and complexity of the task at hand.

The integration of two distinct corporate cultures required more than one person's insight it needed collaboration. As tensions rose between departments and cultures clashed, the senior partner found himself overwhelmed by the sheer volume of issues that needed to be addressed. It was only when he began to rely more on the collective efforts of the team that we began to make headway. Each team member brought something to the table, and together, we found solutions that would have been impossible for any single individual to uncover. This experience solidified for me that no matter how skilled an individual may be, the success of a project depends on a team's ability to communicate, collaborate, and leverage each other's strengths.

Understanding Team Dynamics

A few years later, I worked on a project for a global retail chain. This was a massive undertaking involving teams across three continents, and at the start, it was clear that our efforts were fragmented. Each regional team operated within its silo, tackling problems in isolation. While the local teams worked effectively in their territories, there was little cross-regional collaboration. The lack of cohesion began to hinder our progress, as knowledge and resources weren't being shared effectively across the different teams.

It was then that I looked back to my thoughts on owl colonies. I had observed how these birds maintained loose but effective networks, communicating with each other and exchanging information about hunting grounds and threats to their nests. It struck me that we could adopt a similar approach. Instead of forcing a rigid, centralized structure where every decision had to pass through the top, we could create "collaborative territories." These were areas where each team had autonomy but also clear protocols for sharing information and resources with the other regions.

The change was transformative. Rather than viewing each team as a separate entity, we began to see ourselves as part of a larger ecosystem. A breakthrough discovered in the Asian market would be adapted and improved in Europe and then further refined in North America. This organic sharing of knowledge across teams led to faster, more innovative solutions and allowed us to meet the needs of the client better. By embracing a collaborative framework, we went beyond the limitations of top-down management. The process was not about one team leading all the others; it was about harnessing the collective intelligence of every individual involved. This shift in mindset became the key to our success.

Building Strong Team Foundations

Another pivotal lesson came from a project with a rapidly growing technology start-up. The client needed our help scaling their operations, but the fast-paced environment required that our consulting team expand quickly to meet their evolving needs. Rather than immediately adding more members to the team, we chose to focus on what I like to call "colony strength."

In an owl colony, each member plays a vital role, and the success of the group is contingent on the strength of its foundations. In the same way, we needed to establish clear values and guidelines for how we would work together as a team. First, we defined our core principles. We agreed on the importance of information sharing, mutual support, and an emphasis on collective problem-solving. But just as importantly, we set out to create an environment where each team member could thrive in their way.

Owl colonies are not monolithic; different owls hunt in different areas. Similarly, we recognized that each team member brought a unique skill set to the table. Some of us were better at strategic thinking, while others excelled in data analysis or creative problem-solving. Rather than force everyone into the same mold, we allowed individuals to work in ways that played to their strengths. However, even as we each contributed in our style, we maintained a shared focus on the collective goal.

Integrating new team members was another important step in building our team's strength. Just as new owlets learn from the older, more experienced members of the colony, new members of our consulting team had to be carefully integrated into the existing culture. We didn't just teach them the technical aspects of the job. We helped them understand the implicit rules that governed our collaborative approach. By ensuring that everyone was aligned with the values and principles that defined our teamwork, we created a team that could adapt and evolve without losing sight of the broader vision.

The Art of Team Composition

One of the most crucial lessons I've learned about team effectiveness came from a failed project early in my career. We had assembled a team of brilliant individuals, each with impressive credentials and experience. Yet, the project struggled. The problem wasn't individual capability. It was team composition.

Now, when building consulting teams, I think about the different roles needed for success. Like an owl colony that benefits from members with different strengths and hunting strategies, effective consulting teams need diverse skills and perspectives.

A recent healthcare transformation project illustrated this perfectly. We needed strategic thinkers to envision the future state, detail-oriented analysts to crunch the numbers, relationship builders to manage stakeholder expectations, and pragmatic implementers to make changes happen on the ground. Success came not just from having these different skills but also from how they complemented each other.

Creating Team Synergy

Working with a financial services firm showed me that team synergy isn't accidental; it's carefully cultivated. We faced a challenging situation in which team members had strong, often conflicting views about the best approach. Instead of suppressing these differences, we created what I call "constructive tension zones."

These were structured spaces where team members could safely disagree and debate ideas. Like owl colonies that maintain both individual territories and shared hunting grounds, we balanced individual autonomy with collective decision-making. This approach led to better solutions than any individual team member could have developed alone.

The Role of Leadership in Team Development

Leadership in consulting teams requires a delicate balance. During a large-scale organizational transformation project, I learned that effective team leaders are more like colony coordinators than traditional hierarchical managers.

The best leaders I've worked with create environments where team members can thrive while contributing to collective success. They understand when to step in and when to let the team find its solutions. Like the subtle interactions that maintain order in owl colonies, good leadership often involves indirect influence rather than direct control.

One particularly effective leader I worked with spent more time creating connections between team members than directing their activities. She understood that her role was to facilitate collaboration and remove obstacles rather than micromanage the work.

Cultural Intelligence in Team Dynamics

My global consulting work has taught me the importance of cultural intelligence in team effectiveness. During a project spanning offices in New York, Tokyo, and Mumbai, we had to navigate not just different time zones but also different approaches to teamwork and collaboration.

We learned to appreciate how different cultures view hierarchy, communication, and decision-making. Rather than imposing a single approach, we created flexible frameworks that could accommodate these differences while maintaining project coherence.

This required developing what I call "cultural translation skills" – the ability to understand and bridge different working styles and communication preferences. Like owl colonies that adapt their behaviors to different environments, successful global teams learn to flex their approaches while maintaining their essential character.

Remote Team Collaboration

The recent shift toward remote work has added new dimensions to team dynamics. During a recent digital transformation project, our team was entirely virtual, spread across seven countries. We had to reimagine how to create the kind of spontaneous collaboration that traditionally happened in person.

We developed virtual collaboration spaces that mimicked the natural interaction patterns of owl colonies. These included formal "hunting grounds" for focused work sessions and informal "gathering spots" for casual interaction and idea sharing.

The key was creating multiple channels for interaction while maintaining clear purposes for each. We found that too much structure stifled collaboration, while too little led to confusion and inefficiency.

Managing Team Energy

One often overlooked aspect of team effectiveness is energy management. Like owl colonies that coordinate their activities to maintain constant coverage of their territory, consulting teams need to manage their collective energy efficiently.

During an intensive strategy project, we implemented what I call "energy rotation," deliberately varying the intensity of work across different team members and subgroups. This prevented burnout while maintaining high productivity levels for the team as a whole.

We also learned to recognize and respond to team energy patterns. Some team members were most effective early in the day, others late at night. By understanding and working with these natural rhythms, we improved both productivity and team morale.

Conflict Resolution in Teams

Conflict is inevitable in high-performing teams. A project with a pharmaceutical company taught me valuable lessons about handling team disagreements constructively. Like owl colonies that maintain harmony through established protocols, effective teams need clear mechanisms for resolving conflicts.

We developed a three-level approach to conflict resolution:

- **Direct Conversation:** Encouraging team members to address issues directly with each other first.

- **Mediated Discussion:** Bringing in a neutral third party when direct conversation isn't sufficient.
- **Structural Solution:** Making systemic changes when conflicts reveal underlying team design issues.

Knowledge Sharing and Team Learning

Effective teams, like successful owl colonies, develop sophisticated systems for sharing knowledge and learning from experience. During a long-term transformation project with an insurance company, we created what I call "learning loops" – structured ways to capture and share insights across the team.

These included regular reflection sessions, during which team members shared successes and failures, documentation of key learnings, and mechanisms for incorporating these insights into future work. The key was making knowledge sharing a natural part of daily work rather than a separate activity.

Team Resilience and Adaptation

The most successful teams I've worked with develop strong resilience and the ability to maintain effectiveness even when facing unexpected challenges. Like owl colonies that adapt to changes in their environment, resilient consulting teams can flex and adjust without losing their essential capabilities.

A project with an automotive company demonstrated this perfectly. When market conditions suddenly changed midway through the engagement, our team needed to pivot our approach rapidly. The strength of our team dynamics allowed us to make this shift while maintaining momentum and morale.

Building Team Legacy

One aspect of team effectiveness that often gets overlooked is what I call "legacy building," which creates a lasting impact beyond the current project. Like owl colonies that maintain and improve their territories over generations, great consulting teams build capabilities and relationships that benefit future work.

Working with a consumer goods company, we deliberately structured our team to include both experienced consultants and newer members. This created natural mentoring relationships and helped build the next generation of consulting talent.

The Future of Consulting Teams

As the consulting industry evolves, team structures and dynamics will continue to change. Technology is enabling new forms of collaboration while changing client expectations requires more flexible and adaptive team structures.

Future success will require:

- **Fluid Team Structures:** The ability to quickly form and reform teams based on changing needs.
- **Enhanced Digital Collaboration:** Better tools and protocols for virtual teamwork.
- **Cultural Adaptability:** Increased capability to work effectively across cultural boundaries.

The Colony Advantage

The success of owl colonies offers powerful lessons for consulting teams. Like these remarkable birds, effective teams combine individual excellence with sophisticated collaboration. They develop systems for sharing knowledge, maintaining harmony, and adapting to change.

As you develop your consulting career, remember that your success will depend not just on your capabilities but on your ability to work effectively as part of a team. Like the owls that have mastered the art of colonial living while maintaining their hunting prowess, great consultants learn to balance individual excellence with team collaboration.

The next time you face a challenging project, think about how owl colonies thrive through mutual support and shared purpose. This perspective might just help you transform your team dynamics and achieve better results than any individual effort could produce.

Building and Nurturing Effective Teams in Consulting

The rain pounded against the windows of our Tokyo office as I faced one of the most challenging moments of my consulting career. Our team, assembled from three different continents, was struggling to gel. Despite individual brilliance, we weren't achieving the collective performance our client needed. As I watched raindrops trace patterns on the glass, I remembered how owl colonies successfully integrated new members into their groups, maintaining harmony while maximizing collective effectiveness.

The Art of Team Building

Years ago, I joined a project that seemed perfect on paper. The client, a global manufacturing company, had approved a substantial budget for their digital transformation. We had assembled a team of top consultants, each with impressive credentials. Yet three months in, we were behind schedule and over budget. The problem wasn't individual capability. It was how we functioned as a unit.

This experience taught me that building effective consulting teams requires more than just gathering talented individuals. It demands careful attention to team composition, culture, and development. Just as owl colonies maintain specific social structures that enable collective success, consulting teams need thoughtful design and nurturing to achieve their potential.

Creating the Foundation

Working with a healthcare provider taught me the importance of establishing strong foundations for team success. Like owl colonies that carefully select and prepare their nesting sites, consulting teams need proper groundwork before they can thrive.

Our first step was defining clear team principles. These weren't just generic values posted on a wall. They were specific behaviors and expectations that would guide our daily interactions. We established how decisions would be made, how conflicts would be resolved, and how we would support each other during challenging times.

The principles included commitments to open communication, mutual support, and collective problem-solving. More importantly, we created specific examples of how these principles would manifest in daily work. For instance, "open communication" meant team members would share both successes and struggles during daily stand-ups, making it safe to admit challenges and ask for help.

Integrating New Members

A project with a financial services firm showed me the importance of thoughtful onboarding. New team members, regardless of their experience level, need careful integration into the team's culture and working patterns.

We developed what I call the "partnership model" for integrating new team members. Each newcomer was paired with an experienced team member who served as both a guide and advocate. This partnership went beyond simple mentoring it was a two-way relationship where both parties could learn from each other.

The system helped new members understand not just their tasks but also the unwritten rules and cultural nuances that often determine success in consulting teams. It also provided a safe space for questions and concerns that might not surface in larger group settings.

Nurturing Team Growth

During a long-term transformation project with a retail chain, I learned that team development is an ongoing process, not a one-time event. Like owl colonies that continuously adapt their behaviors and relationships, consulting teams need constant attention and nurturing.

We instituted regular team development sessions that went beyond typical project updates. These sessions focused on how we worked together, addressing both successes and challenges in our collaboration. The key was creating a safe space where team members could openly discuss interpersonal dynamics without fear of judgment.

One particularly effective practice was what we called "appreciation rounds." Team members would share specific examples of how others had helped them succeed. This not only boosted morale but also highlighted effective collaborative behaviors that others could emulate.

Managing Team Dynamics

A technology project in Silicon Valley taught me about managing the complex dynamics that emerge in high-performance teams. We had brilliant individuals who were used to being the smartest person in the room. The challenge was channeling their expertise while maintaining team harmony.

We implemented what I call "dynamic role rotation." Team members would take turns leading different aspects of the project, forcing them to alternate between leading and supporting roles. This approach helped break down ego barriers and build mutual respect among team members.

The system also helped identify hidden strengths in team members. Someone who might seem quiet in group settings could shine when leading their area of expertise. This rotating leadership model created a more balanced team dynamic where everyone had opportunities to lead and follow.

Developing Collective Intelligence

Working with an aerospace company showed me how teams can develop collective intelligence that surpasses individual expertise. Like owl colonies that share information about hunting grounds and potential threats, effective consulting teams create systems for pooling and leveraging collective knowledge.

We established regular knowledge-sharing sessions in which team members taught others about their areas of expertise. These weren't formal presentations but interactive discussions in which everyone could contribute insights and ask questions.

The key was creating an environment where people felt comfortable sharing both knowledge and uncertainty. We encouraged team members to present not just their successes but also their challenges and open questions. This vulnerability paradoxically strengthened the team's collective capability.

Building Remote Team Cohesion

Recent years have taught us much about building team cohesion in remote settings. During a global strategy project, our team was spread across five time zones. We had to reimagine how to create the kind of team spirit that traditionally developed through in-person interaction.

We developed what I call "virtual touch points" structured opportunities for team connection that went beyond project work. These included virtual coffee chats, online team games, and digital celebration moments. The key was making these interactions feel natural rather than forced.

One particularly successful initiative was our "digital water cooler," an always-open video channel where team members could drop in for informal conversations. This created opportunities for the spontaneous interactions that often drive team cohesion.

Managing Team Energy

Long-term consulting projects can be exhausting, and maintaining team energy requires deliberate effort. Working with a pharmaceutical company during a complex regulatory change, I learned the importance of energy management at both individual and team levels.

We implemented an energy rotation system that balanced intense work periods with recovery time. Team members alternated between high-intensity project phases and lighter support roles, ensuring sustainable performance over the long term.

The system included regular check-ins about energy levels and workload distribution. We made it acceptable to admit when you needed a break and created processes for redistributing work when necessary.

Cultivating Team Resilience

In the world of consulting, the journey is often marked by uncertainty and rapid change. This is especially true in industries that face external challenges like market downturns, technological disruptions, or shifts in consumer behavior. These factors often create environments where teams must not only survive but thrive amidst adversity. One of my most profound learning experiences regarding team resilience came during a project with an automotive manufacturer navigating a significant industry downturn. Through this project, I came to understand the critical role resilience plays in maintaining team effectiveness in the face of external pressure.

As we entered this engagement, the automotive sector was grappling with declining demand, tightening budgets, and rapidly changing consumer preferences. The atmosphere was thick with anxiety, and the uncertainty surrounding the project was palpable. The client was facing multiple setbacks, and the internal team of consultants was feeling the weight of these challenges. It was clear that we needed to adopt a new approach one that would allow us not only to persevere but also continue to perform at a high level despite the numerous obstacles.

I realized that cultivating resilience within the team would be the key to maintaining performance and morale. In this context, resilience wasn't just about bouncing back from setbacks; it was about building an ongoing capacity to handle setbacks, adapt to new circumstances, and emerge stronger with each challenge faced. Resilience had to become part of the team's DNA.

Building this resilience was not instantaneous. It required a fundamental shift in how we approached difficulties and setbacks, both individually and collectively. We needed to recognize that challenges and obstacles were inevitable and that they were not a sign of failure but a natural part of the consulting journey. This mindset shift allowed us to start building what I now refer to as **"resilience rituals."**

Resilience Rituals

At its core, **resilience rituals** were regular, structured practices that kept the team grounded and focused during periods of uncertainty. They became our anchor, our routine in the chaos. One of the first practices we implemented was a weekly reflection session. These sessions were designed to provide the team with a dedicated space to discuss the challenges faced during the week openly, reflect on how we responded to those challenges, and share any small wins, no matter how insignificant they might seem.

The reflection sessions became a powerful tool for boosting morale. In an environment where setbacks were frequent and progress often slow, these sessions provided the team with an opportunity to pause and celebrate even the smallest victories. Whether it was solving a complex problem, landing a difficult client meeting, or overcoming a technical roadblock, these moments of success were acknowledged and celebrated. Over time, these rituals helped shift the team's mindset, making it easier for them to keep going even when things seemed overwhelming.

In addition to reflection sessions, we also implemented **support mechanisms** tailored to individual team members facing specific challenges. Consulting is a high-pressure field, and inevitably, the stress of a difficult project will particularly impact certain members. These support mechanisms involved pairing individuals with mentors, creating opportunities for peer coaching, and ensuring that each person had access to resources that would help them manage their workload and stress levels. This support structure allowed team members to feel that they were not alone in their struggles. It also fostered a sense of community within the group, which was crucial to maintaining morale.

It became clear that the true value of these resilience rituals lay not in any one specific practice but in the consistency and frequency of these efforts. By integrating resilience-building practices into our weekly routine, we ensured that no one felt isolated, overwhelmed, or unsupported. The rituals became a source of strength, helping the team navigate the tough days with a renewed sense of purpose.

Normalizing Setbacks as Part of the Journey
One of the hardest lessons we had to learn was how to normalize setbacks. In the consulting world, there is often an overwhelming drive to perform flawlessly, to meet client expectations at every turn, and to deliver results on time and budget. While these are important goals, they can also create an environment where even small mistakes are seen as catastrophic. This tendency toward perfectionism can be toxic, and it was clear that it had to change if the team was going to remain resilient.

Through open communication and the reinforcement of the **resilience rituals**, we began to shift the team's perspective. Setbacks were not signs of failure but rather opportunities to learn, adapt, and grow. This reframing was instrumental in cultivating a more resilient mindset within the team. Rather than allowing mistakes to derail progress, we used them as stepping stones toward improvement. We took the time to analyze what went wrong, extract lessons, and make adjustments for the future. Over time, this approach became ingrained in our culture, and the team developed an increasing sense of comfort with uncertainty.

As we progressed through the project, we saw the power of this mindset shift in action. The team began to handle stress more effectively, maintaining a sense of calm and composure even in the face of unexpected challenges. Setbacks no longer paralyzed them; instead, they embraced them as part of the learning process. The resilience rituals became so deeply embedded in our routine that they became second nature, and the team's ability to handle adversity grew stronger with each passing week.

The Owl Colony Analogy

To reinforce this message of resilience, I often used the analogy of owl colonies. In the wild, owls are known for their ability to adapt to difficult environments. Despite facing harsh weather, limited resources, and other challenges, owl colonies continue to function effectively. Their success is not due to the absence of challenges but because of their ability to cope with them collectively.

In the same way, a consulting team must be able to navigate difficulties together, drawing strength from one another. Each team member, like an owl in the colony, has a unique role and perspective that contributes to the collective resilience. The key to survival, both for owl colonies and consulting teams, is interdependence. In our case, it was regular reflection, shared learning from setbacks, and ongoing support for one another that allowed us to remain effective during adversity.

Much like owl colonies that thrive in spite of environmental challenges, consulting teams that develop resilience rituals are better equipped to handle the pressures of an unpredictable world. By normalizing setbacks, providing consistent support, and fostering a culture of continuous learning, teams can build the kind of resilience that will allow them to weather even the toughest storms.

CHAPTER 6
LEADING WITH VISION

S arah stood at the window of her corner office, gazing at the Manhattan skyline as the sun dipped below the horizon. After fifteen years in management consulting, she learned that true leadership wasn't about having all the answers. It was about asking the right questions and inspiring others to find innovative solutions. The path that led her here hadn't been straight or easy, but it had taught her invaluable lessons about leading with vision.

Lessons from Alpha Owls: Guiding the Flock

The Essence of Visionary Leadership

In the dense forest of management consulting, being merely skilled isn't enough. True leadership emerges from those who can see beyond the immediate landscape, much like the alpha owl perched atop the highest branch, surveying both the details below and the broader horizon ahead. This chapter delves into the art of visionary leadership in consulting, drawing parallel wisdom from nature's most strategic nocturnal hunters.

Consider Sarah Chen, a senior partner at one of the Big Three consulting firms, who transformed a struggling telecommunications client by envisioning their pivot to digital services five years before the market demanded it. "Leadership isn't about having all the answers," she reflects, "it's about seeing the patterns others miss and having the courage to guide your team toward that distant point on the horizon."

The Architecture of Strategic Foresight

Just as alpha owls possess specialized neck vertebrae that allow them to rotate their heads 270 degrees, successful consulting leaders must develop a comprehensive view of their environment. This involves three critical dimensions: temporal vision (past, present, future), spatial awareness (market dynamics, competitive landscapes), and stakeholder perception (client needs, team capabilities, market demands).

David Morrison, a veteran consultant with twenty years of experience, shares a pivotal moment from his career: "I was leading a manufacturing transformation project when I noticed subtle shifts in raw material pricing patterns. While others focused on immediate cost-cutting, I guided my team to develop a revolutionary supply chain model that anticipated market changes. That project not only saved the client $50 million annually but positioned them as industry innovators."

Cultivating the Alpha Mindset

Leadership in consulting requires more than traditional management skills. It demands the development of what we call the "Alpha Owl Mindset," a unique combination of attributes that elevate a consultant from being merely competent to truly visionary:

The first pillar is Anticipatory Intelligence. Like the owl's ability to detect the slightest movement in complete darkness, successful consulting leaders must develop an almost supernatural ability to sense market shifts and emerging opportunities. This involves constant environmental scanning, pattern recognition, and the courage to act on insights before they become obvious to others.

James Whitaker, CEO of a boutique consulting firm specializing in tech transformation, explains: "I train my consultants to spend 20% of their time exploring weak signals, those barely perceptible changes in customer behavior, technological advancement, or regulatory environment that could reshape entire industries. It's not about predicting the future; it's about being prepared to adapt and guide others when change arrives."

The Power of Strategic Silence

One of the most overlooked aspects of leadership in consulting is knowing when to maintain strategic silence. Just as owls hunt with absolute stealth, effective leaders understand the power of calculated restraint. This doesn't mean being passive; rather, it's about creating space for team insights to emerge and client perspectives to surface.

Maria Gonzalez, a transformation specialist, shares her experience: "In a critical strategy session with a Fortune 500 client, I noticed the tendency of junior consultants to fill every silence with suggestions. Instead, I implemented what I call 'strategic pause points' designated moments of reflection that allowed deeper insights to emerge. This approach led to the client team identifying critical implementation challenges we might have missed in a more conventional discussion."

Building High-Performance Teams

Like alpha owls who ensure the survival and success of their entire flock, consulting leaders must excel at building and nurturing high-performance teams. This involves several key elements:

Vision Alignment: Every team member must understand not just the what and how but the why behind strategic decisions. This deeper understanding enables consultants to make better autonomous decisions and maintain project momentum even in the leader's absence.

Capability Development: True leaders invest in developing their team's capabilities across multiple dimensions. This includes technical skills, client management abilities, and strategic thinking capacity. The goal is to create a team of future leaders, not just efficient executors.

Navigating Through Complexity

The modern consulting landscape resembles a labyrinth of interconnected challenges, where every decision ripples through multiple dimensions of business operations. Like the alpha owl's ability to navigate through darkness, today's consulting leaders must guide their teams through unprecedented levels of complexity.

Consider the experience of Thomas Chang, who led a digital transformation project for a global retail chain: "We faced a scenario where technological advancement, changing consumer behavior, and supply chain disruptions created a perfect storm of complexity. The key wasn't simplifying the complexity – it was developing frameworks that allowed us to navigate through it while maintaining strategic clarity."

The Art of Strategic Communication

Communication in consulting leadership transcends mere information transfer. It's an art form that requires masterful execution across multiple levels:

- Upward Communication: Leaders must articulate vision and progress to senior stakeholders and clients in a way that builds confidence while maintaining transparency about challenges. This involves what veteran consultant Rebecca Foster calls "strategic framing" – presenting complex situations in ways that highlight both challenges and opportunities without overwhelming decision-makers.

- Horizontal Communication: Engaging with peers and partner organizations requires a delicate balance of collaboration and competitive awareness. Mark Stevens, a senior partner specializing in cross-industry transformations, shares: "I've learned to create what I call 'collaborative boundaries' frameworks that enable productive partnership while protecting proprietary insights and methodologies."

- Downward Communication: The most crucial aspect of leadership communication involves inspiring and guiding team members. This requires a combination of clarity, authenticity, and strategic timing. "I've found that the most effective leaders don't just communicate plans and expectations," notes Dr. Sarah Williams, a leadership development expert, "they create a narrative that team members can see themselves in."

Leading Through Crisis

Crisis management represents perhaps the most critical test of consulting leadership. Like the alpha owl protecting its flock during a storm, leaders must demonstrate both strength and adaptability when facing unexpected challenges.

Michael Chen, who guided several Fortune 500 companies through the global financial crisis, shares his philosophy: "Crisis leadership in consulting isn't about having all the answers. It's about maintaining strategic clarity while being honest about uncertainties. I've developed what I call the

'Triple A Framework': Acknowledge the reality, Assess the options, and Act with conviction."

The Innovation Imperative

Today's consulting leaders must foster innovation while maintaining operational excellence. This dual requirement demands a unique approach to leadership that balances creative exploration with practical execution.

Dr. Elena Rodriguez, known for pioneering new approaches to strategic transformation, explains: "Innovation in consulting isn't just about generating new ideas. It's about creating an environment where innovative thinking becomes part of the team's DNA while maintaining the rigor and reliability our clients expect."

Developing Future Leaders

Perhaps the most critical responsibility of consulting leaders is nurturing the next generation of visionary guides. This involves several key dimensions:

Mentorship Architecture: Creating structured yet flexible frameworks for developing future leaders. Victoria Wu, global head of talent development at a leading consulting firm, shares: "We've moved beyond traditional mentorship models to what we call 'dynamic development pods' – small groups of consultants at different experience levels who learn from each other while tackling real client challenges."

Experiential Learning: Providing carefully calibrated exposure to complex situations. "The key is finding the right balance between challenge and support," notes James Mitchell, a veteran consultant turned leadership coach. "Too much protection prevents growth, while too little can break confidence."

The Ethics of Leadership

In an era of increased scrutiny and stakeholder expectations, consulting leaders must navigate complex ethical landscapes while maintaining business effectiveness. This requires developing what Dr. Amanda Thompson calls "ethical intelligence" the ability to anticipate and address moral challenges before they become crises.

The Digital Transformation Imperative

In today's consulting landscape, digital transformation isn't just a service offering it's a leadership imperative. Like the alpha owl adapting its hunting techniques to changing environments, consulting leaders must master the digital realm while maintaining their strategic essence.

Patricia Zhao, who leads digital transformation initiatives across Asia-Pacific, shares: "The challenge isn't just understanding technology; it's about maintaining human connection and strategic insight while leveraging digital capabilities. We've developed what I call 'hybrid leadership' combining traditional consulting wisdom with digital fluency."

Global Leadership Dynamics

Modern consulting leaders must navigate an increasingly interconnected global business environment. This requires developing what Dr. Richard Torres terms "cultural intelligence quotient" the ability to lead effectively across diverse cultural contexts while maintaining strategic consistency.

The Sustainability Mandate

Environmental, Social, and Governance (ESG) considerations have become central to consulting leadership. Alexandra Kim, who specializes in sustainable transformation, explains: "Today's leaders must integrate sustainability into every aspect of strategic thinking. It's no longer an add-on; it's fundamental to long-term value creation."

Building Resilient Organizations

The concept of resilience has evolved beyond mere risk management. Modern consulting leaders must help organizations develop what Dr. Marcus Chen calls "adaptive resilience" the ability to not just survive disruption but thrive through it.

The Future of Consulting Leadership

As we look ahead, several key trends are reshaping the landscape of consulting leadership:

- **Artificial Intelligence Integration:** Leaders must understand how to leverage AI while maintaining the human elements that drive successful consulting engagements. Dr. Sarah Hayes, an AI strategy expert, notes: "The future belongs to leaders who can orchestrate the perfect symphony between human insight and machine capability."

- **Ecosystem Leadership:** The ability to lead across increasingly complex partner networks becomes crucial. "Traditional organizational boundaries are blurring," observes Michael O'Connor, global alliance director at a leading firm. "Tomorrow's leaders must excel at orchestrating value creation across entire ecosystems."

Personal Leadership Development

The journey to becoming a visionary consulting leader requires continuous personal development. This involves:

Self-Reflection: Regular assessment of leadership style and impact. Adaptive Learning: Continuously updating skills and knowledge. Energy Management: Maintaining personal resilience and effectiveness

The Legacy Dimension

True consulting leaders think beyond immediate project success to consider their long-term impact on their profession, their teams, and their clients. Dr. Jennifer Liu, author of "The Consulting Legacy," shares: "The measure of a consulting leader isn't just in the problems solved but, in the capabilities, built and the wisdom transferred."

Strategies for fostering innovation and purpose.

Creating an Innovation Ecosystem

A consulting leader's ability to foster innovation determines their team's long-term success. Karen Chen, innovation director at McKinsey, transformed her practice by establishing what she calls "innovation zones," dedicated spaces and times where consultants can explore unconventional solutions without immediate pressure for results.

Building Innovation Capabilities

Innovation in consulting requires systematic development across three dimensions:

- Cognitive flexibility: the ability to reframe problems and see new patterns. David Liu implemented a "perspective rotation" program where consultants regularly switch between industries to cross-pollinate ideas. "Our healthcare team's breakthrough in patient flow management came from studying airport logistics," he notes.

- Technical adaptability, staying current with emerging tools and methodologies. The Boston Consulting Group's Digital Innovation Lab demonstrates this through its "tech immersion sprints," where consulting teams spend intensive periods mastering new technologies alongside client implementation.

- Collaborative innovation the ability to co-create solutions with clients and partners. "Innovation isn't something we do to clients, but with them," explains

Maria Stevenson, who pioneered Deloitte's client innovation workshops.

Purpose Driven Consulting

Purpose transforms consulting from a service into a mission. Sarah Thompson revolutionized her practice by aligning each project with broader societal impact: "We measure success not just in ROI, but in sustainable value creation across stakeholder groups."

Innovation Metrics and Incentives

Traditional consulting metrics often stifle innovation. Progressive firms are adopting new measurement systems:

Impact Scoring: Evaluating innovations based on client transformation potential rather than just immediate results. Learning Metrics: Tracking team capability development alongside project outcomes. Sustainability Indicators: Measuring long-term value creation across environmental and social dimensions

The Innovation-Purpose Connection

The most successful consulting leaders integrate innovation and purpose through:

- Strategic alignment between innovation initiatives and broader societal needs
- Development of solutions that address both business and social challenges
- Creation of measurement frameworks that capture multiple forms of value creation

Fostering a Culture of Purposeful Innovation

Innovation in consulting must transcend traditional brainstorming sessions and ideation workshops. Andrew Chen, transformation lead at Bain, revolutionized his practice by implementing what he calls "purpose-driven innovation sprints," intensive periods where teams tackle specific client challenges while maintaining focus on broader societal impact.

The Innovation Leadership Framework

Successful consulting leaders follow a structured approach to fostering innovation:

- **Vision Setting:** Creating compelling narratives that connect immediate client needs with long-term transformation potential. Rachel Martinez shares: "We begin each engagement by asking not just 'what needs to change?' but 'What future are we creating?'"

- **Capability Building**: Developing teams' capacity for innovative thinking through structured programs. The "Innovation Academy" at McKinsey demonstrates this approach, combining technical training with creative problem-solving exercises.

Creating Safe Spaces for Experimentation

Innovation requires psychological safety and the confidence to propose unconventional solutions without fear of ridicule or repercussion. Michael Chang established "innovation sandboxes" where teams can test radical ideas before client presentations: "We celebrate failed experiments as learning opportunities."

Purpose as an Innovation Catalyst

Purpose drives innovation by:
- Providing clear direction for creative efforts
- Inspiring teams to push beyond conventional solutions
- Attracting and retaining top talent aligned with organizational values

Dr. Elena Rodriguez explains: "When consultants understand the broader purpose of their work, they naturally push boundaries and seek transformative solutions."

Cross-Pollination and Knowledge Transfer

Leading firms are breaking down traditional practice silos to foster innovation:

- Regular rotation of consultants across industries
- Cross-functional innovation teams
- Client-consultant innovation labs

PART 4: PATIENCE & LONG-TERM THINKING

CHAPTER 7
THE WAITING GAME

Owls' Patience in Predatory Success

Management consulting, much like the silent hunt of the wise owl, often demands a calculated patience that many find challenging to master. The consulting industry is brimming with ambitious professionals eager to deliver solutions and drive impactful change. Yet, true success in consulting is rarely about speed alone. It lies in the ability to wait, observe, and strike only when the time is right. Just as owls are revered for their ability to sit still, blend into their environment, and wait for the perfect moment to pounce, a consultant must cultivate the art of patience to achieve long-term strategic goals.

Understanding Patience as a Strategic Asset

In a world where immediacy is often mistaken for efficiency, patience might seem counterintuitive. However, for management consultants, it is a strategic asset that complements sharp intellect and decisive action. Patience does not imply inaction; instead, it represents the deliberate choice to pause, reflect, and understand the intricate web of dynamics at play before executing a solution.

Consider the owl perched silently on a branch, surveying its surroundings. It observes not only its prey but the broader environment, twin direction, movements of other animals, and the perfect angle for attack. Similarly, a consultant must develop the ability to analyze the external and internal forces shaping a client's ecosystem. By practicing patience, consultants can avoid knee-jerk reactions and instead deliver strategies that address the root of a problem rather than its symptoms.

In the consulting world, patience manifests in various ways:

- Waiting for the right timing to propose transformative ideas.
- Allowing clients to absorb initial recommendations before implementing new changes.
- Observing team dynamics and company culture to craft solutions that align with organizational values.

The Role of Observation in Patience

Patience and observation are inseparable. Without a keen sense of observation, patience devolves into mere passivity. The owl's success is deeply rooted in its observational prowess. It sees what others cannot, notices the smallest shifts in its surroundings, and processes this data to make calculated moves.

As a consultant, developing observational skills means more than simply gathering data or attending client meetings. It involves reading between the lines, understanding unspoken concerns, and recognizing opportunities hidden beneath surface-level challenges.

- **Client Behavior**: Every client interaction provides subtle cues. A hesitance to embrace change might indicate a deeper fear of organizational disruption. Being patient and observant allows you to detect these signals and address them tactfully.
- **Market Trends**: Markets, like ecosystems, operate on their rhythms. Observing emerging trends and understanding their implications can position you as a forward-thinking advisor.

- **Competitor Strategies**: By patiently monitoring competitors' movements, consultants can help clients pre-empt disruptions and capitalize on market gaps.

One of the greatest mistakes in consulting is rushing to present solutions without fully grasping the nuances of a situation. Just as the owl waits for its prey to align perfectly within its sight, consultants must learn to wait for the right alignment of circumstances before advising action.

Case Study: The Power of Waiting in Client Engagements

Let's take an example from real-world consulting to highlight the importance of patience.

A mid-sized manufacturing company approached a consulting firm to help streamline its supply chain processes. At first glance, the problem seemed to stem from inefficient supplier contracts and outdated logistics. A less experienced consultant might have jumped straight into renegotiating contracts and implementing new logistics software.

However, a senior consultant on the team advocated for a deeper, more patient approach. Over three months, the consulting team closely observed the company's operations, held multiple stakeholder interviews, and analyzed historical data. What they discovered was surprising: the inefficiencies were not due to external suppliers but internal communication gaps between the procurement and operations teams. The solution involved restructuring team workflows and improving inter-departmental collaboration, a strategy that saved the company millions in the long term.

Had the team rushed into action without waiting to uncover the real issue, their solution would have been misaligned with the company's needs. This case underscores the value of patience in identifying and addressing the root causes of complex challenges.

Balancing Urgency and Patience

Patience does not mean neglecting urgency. On the contrary, the best consultants know how to balance the two. Urgency is essential when addressing immediate client needs or mitigating risks. However, urgency should never compromise the thoroughness of your approach.

Striking this balance requires:

- **Setting Clear Priorities**: Differentiate between what needs immediate attention and what can benefit from further analysis.
- **Managing Client Expectations**: Clients often expect quick results, but it is your role to communicate the benefits of a measured approach.
- **Maintaining Momentum**: Patience should not lead to stagnation. Ensure progress is made even as you wait for the right moment to implement major changes.

The wise owl, though patient, is always alert and ready to act. Similarly, consultants must remain active, engaged, and prepared to seize opportunities when they arise.

The Long-Term View: Building Credibility Through Patience

Patience is not just about achieving immediate success; it's about building credibility and trust over the long term. Clients value consultants who demonstrate a commitment to understanding their unique challenges and delivering tailored solutions. By exercising patience, you show clients that their goals are your priority and that you are invested in their success beyond the scope of a single project.

In many ways, patience is a test of character. It requires discipline, humility, and a willingness to put the client's needs above your desire for quick wins. Over time, this approach not only strengthens client relationships but also enhances your reputation as a thoughtful, strategic consultant.

Patience as the Foundation of Long-Term Strategies

One of the greatest lessons consultants can learn from the owl is that success often requires a long-term perspective. The owl's patience is not passive; it is deeply intentional. Every moment of stillness serves a purpose: gathering information, calculating risk, and ensuring the conditions are optimal for success. Similarly, long-term strategies in management consulting hinge on the ability to be deliberate and purposeful in every decision.

For consultants, this means resisting the urge to prioritize short-term wins at the expense of sustainable impact. Quick fixes might earn temporary praise, but they rarely deliver the transformative results clients expect. To truly excel in the consulting world, you must think beyond immediate solutions and craft strategies that account for the future.

Why Long-Term Thinking Matters in Consulting

- **Navigating Complexity**: Most consulting projects involve intricate challenges that cannot be resolved overnight. For example, restructuring an organization or entering a new market requires detailed planning and time to anticipate and mitigate unforeseen challenges.

- **Building Resilience**: Long-term strategies ensure that clients are prepared to adapt to changes in their industry, whether those changes come from technological advancements, economic shifts, or competitive pressures.

- **Earning Trust**: Clients value consultants who demonstrate foresight and are willing to invest time in crafting solutions that truly serve their interests. By focusing on the long term, you establish yourself as a partner in their success rather than a vendor delivering a quick service.

A patient, strategic approach sets the stage for sustainable growth and positions both the consultant and the client for lasting success.

Timing Is Everything: Recognizing the Perfect Moment to Act

One of the most challenging aspects of consulting is knowing when to move from observation to action. This moment when patience transitions into decisive action can make or break a project's success. Just as an owl waits for its prey to be within striking distance, consultants must learn to recognize when the conditions are ripe for implementing change.

Timing in consulting is nuanced. It requires an understanding of external factors, such as market trends or regulatory shifts, and an acute awareness of internal dynamics within the client organization. Acting too soon can lead to resistance or incomplete solutions while waiting too long can cause missed opportunities.

Key Indicators That the Time Is Right

- **Alignment Among Stakeholders**: Successful implementation often depends on buy-in from key stakeholders. Patience allows you to engage these individuals, address their concerns, and build consensus before launching a major initiative.

- **Sufficient Data and Insights**: Decisions should be based on a thorough understanding of the problem.

Waiting for the necessary data, whether financial metrics, customer feedback, or operational benchmarks, ensures that your recommendations are well-informed.

- **Market Readiness**: External conditions play a significant role in timing. For example, launching a new product might depend on seasonal demand, competitor actions, or shifts in consumer behavior.

By honing your ability to read these signals, you can maximize the impact of your strategies and avoid the pitfalls of premature action.

The Psychological Challenges of Waiting

Patience may be a virtue, but it is not always easy to practice, especially in a high-pressure environment like consulting. Consultants are often under immense pressure to deliver results quickly, whether from demanding clients, tight deadlines, or their internal drive for success. The waiting game can feel frustrating or even counterproductive, leading some to take impulsive actions just to feel a sense of progress.

However, it's important to remember that patience is not synonymous with idleness. The waiting period is an active phase of preparation and reflection, during which you refine your strategy and position yourself for success. Overcoming the psychological challenges of waiting requires a combination of mindset shifts and practical techniques:

- **Shift Your Perspective**

Instead of viewing patience as a delay, see it as an investment in the quality of your work. Every moment spent observing, analyzing, and strategizing enhances the effectiveness of your eventual actions.

- **Practice Mindfulness**

Mindfulness techniques, such as meditation or journaling, can help you stay grounded and focused during periods of waiting. By managing stress and maintaining clarity, you'll be better equipped to make sound decisions when the time comes.

- **Break Down the Process**

Large projects can feel overwhelming, especially when progress seems slow. Breaking your strategy into smaller, manageable milestones allows you to celebrate incremental successes and maintain momentum.

- **Trust the Process**

Patience requires confidence in your abilities and the process you've designed. Trusting that your deliberate approach will yield results can help you resist the temptation to rush.

Case Study: Strategic Patience in Market Entry

Consider the example of a multinational corporation looking to expand into a new geographic market. The initial analysis revealed a lucrative opportunity, with high demand for the company's products and limited competition. However, entering the market immediately would have been a mistake, as the regulatory landscape was in flux, and local consumer preferences were not fully understood.

The consulting team recommended a phased approach:

1. **Phase 1**: Conduct in-depth market research to understand local preferences, cultural nuances, and regulatory requirements.
2. **Phase 2**: Establish strategic partnerships with local distributors to build brand presence and gain market insights.
3. **Phase 3**: Launch a pilot program to test the waters before scaling operations.

This patient, step-by-step strategy paid off. By the time the company fully entered the market, it had a clear understanding of customer needs, strong local partnerships, and a regulatory framework that supported its operations. The company's careful approach not only minimized risks but also maximized its long-term potential for growth.

Cultivating Patience in Your Consulting Practice

Developing patience is not an overnight process. Like any skill, it requires practice and conscious effort. To cultivate this trait, consider the following:

- **Learn from Experience**: Reflect on past projects where patience (or the lack thereof) impacted the outcome. What lessons can you apply to future engagements?
- **Seek Mentors**: Experienced consultants often have valuable insights into the art of timing. Learning from their experiences can accelerate your development.
- **Practice Delayed Gratification**: Train yourself to prioritize long-term benefits over immediate rewards, both in your personal life and professional practice.
- **Embrace Uncertainty**: Waiting often involves uncertainty. Developing comfort with ambiguity can help you navigate the waiting game with confidence.

Patience and Adaptability: The Dual Pillars of Success

While patience is a powerful tool, it must be coupled with adaptability to thrive in the ever-changing landscape of management consulting. The owl, though patient, is not rigid. It adjusts its strategy based on environmental shifts, the movement of prey, and external threats. In the same vein, consultants must balance patience with the flexibility to pivot when circumstances demand it.

Why Adaptability Enhances Patience

- **Responding to Evolving Client Needs**: Even during a deliberate waiting phase, clients' priorities can shift. Being adaptable ensures that you remain aligned with their changing goals.
- **Navigating Unforeseen Challenges**: External disruptions, such as market downturns or regulatory changes, can render initial plans obsolete. Patience allows you to pause and reassess, while adaptability ensures you can quickly recalibrate your approach.
- **Seizing Unexpected Opportunities**: Sometimes, waiting reveals opportunities that were not apparent at the outset. Being adaptable allows you to capitalize on these moments without abandoning your overarching strategy.

For example, imagine working with a client in the retail sector during a time of economic uncertainty. While patiently waiting for the right moment to launch a new product, you notice a sudden surge in demand for e-commerce solutions. By adapting your strategy to incorporate digital tools and online marketing, you can help the client pivot effectively and achieve success despite the challenging environment.

The Risks of Impatience in Consulting

Patience may seem challenging, but impatience is far more costly. Rushing into action without adequate preparation often leads to:

- **Superficial Solutions**: Quick fixes might address symptoms of a problem but fail to resolve its underlying causes.
- **Client Dissatisfaction**: Acting hastily can create the impression that you are more focused on speed than quality, eroding trust and credibility.
- **Missed Opportunities**: By moving too quickly, you risk overlooking valuable insights or alternative solutions that could have emerged with more careful observation.

One of the most common pitfalls for new consultants is feeling pressured to deliver results immediately. While it is important to show progress, it is equally critical to manage expectations and communicate the value of a thoughtful, patient approach.

Real World Example: Impatience Gone Wrong

A global technology company once hired a consulting firm to help with a major organizational restructuring. The firm, eager to impress, rushed into recommending widespread layoffs and the introduction of a new operational model.

However, the consultants failed to take the time to fully understand the company's culture and the loyalty employees felt toward their leadership. The layoffs caused a public relations backlash, and the operational changes faced significant resistance from the remaining workforce.

In hindsight, a more patient approach focusing first on building internal alignment and conducting a phased implementation could have achieved the same goals with far less disruption. This example serves as a cautionary tale of how impatience can undermine even the best intentions.

Patience as a Competitive Advantage

In an industry as competitive as management consulting, patience can set you apart from your peers. While others focus on delivering rapid results, a consultant who takes the time to understand a client's unique needs and craft a tailored strategy often earns greater respect and loyalty.

Ways Patience Enhances Your Competitive Edge

- **Stronger Client Relationships**: Patience demonstrates your commitment to the client's success, fostering trust and long-term partnerships.
- **Deeper Insights**: The more time you spend observing and analyzing, the more nuanced your understanding of the problem becomes. This leads to more innovative and impactful solutions.
- **Resilience in the Face of Challenges**: Patience allows you to weather setbacks and maintain focus on the ultimate goal, even when progress feels slow.

Consider the wise owl again. It doesn't rush into the hunt, even when hungry. Its ability to wait and act only when the conditions are optimal ensures its survival. Similarly, patience is not just a skill but a strategy that can give you a significant advantage in the consulting world.

The Art of Communicating Patience to Clients

One of the biggest challenges consultants face is convincing clients of the value of patience. Many clients expect immediate results driven by internal pressures or external stakeholders. To navigate this, you must be skilled in articulating why a deliberate approach is in their best interest.

Strategies for Effective Communication

- **Set Expectations Early**: From the outset of a project, explain the rationale behind your timeline and how patience will lead to better outcomes.
- **Show Progress Along the Way**: Even during waiting periods, provide updates that highlight the work being done, whether it's data analysis, stakeholder interviews, or market research.
- **Use Analogies and Stories**: Drawing parallels to relatable scenarios, such as the owl's hunting strategy, can help clients understand the value of waiting for the right moment.
- **Highlight the Risks of Rushing**: Use case studies or examples to illustrate how impatience can lead to suboptimal results.

The ability to convey the importance of patience not only helps clients buy into your approach but also reinforces your credibility as a thoughtful and strategic advisor.

Lessons from the Wise Owl: Applying Patience to Your Career

Patience is essential for achieving consulting goals and navigating one's career as a consultant. Success in this field rarely happens overnight. Building a reputation, developing expertise, and cultivating a strong professional network all require time and perseverance.

Applying Patience to Career Growth

- **Master Your Craft**: Develop a deep understanding of your industry and refine your consulting skills.
- **Build Meaningful Relationships**: Networking is not about collecting business cards—it's about nurturing genuine connections over time.
- **Embrace Continuous Learning**: The consulting landscape is constantly evolving. Staying patient and open to learning ensures you remain relevant and adaptable.
- **Measure Success Over the Long Term**: Instead of focusing solely on short-term achievements, evaluate

your career based on the impact you've made and the relationships you've built.

Just as the owl's patience ensures its survival, your ability to wait, observe, and act deliberately will position you for lasting success in your consulting career.

Embracing the Waiting Game

Patience is not merely a skill. It is a mindset and a philosophy that underpins every aspect of successful consulting. By learning to wait with purpose, observe with intention, and act with precision, you can unlock the full potential of your 360-degree wise owl.

The waiting game may test your resolve, but it also hones your ability to think strategically, build trust, and deliver results that stand the test of time. As you continue your journey in the consulting world, remember the lesson of the owl: patience is not a weakness; it is a superpower that sets you apart as a thoughtful, strategic, and impactful advisor.

CHAPTER 8
THRIVING UNDER PRESSURE

The gleaming office windows of a Fortune 500 company reflect the early morning sun as Sarah Martinez, a senior consultant at McKinsey, takes a deep breath before entering the building. In her briefcase lies the strategic transformation proposal that could either revolutionize the client's operations or become a costly misstep. The weight of this responsibility isn't unique to Sarah. It's a daily reality for management consultants worldwide.

Pressure in consulting isn't just about deadlines and deliverables; it's an intricate web of expectations, relationships, and high-stakes decisions that can make or break careers and companies alike. Understanding the psychological landscape of pressure is crucial for any consultant aiming to thrive rather than merely survive in this demanding profession.

The human brain responds to consulting pressure in fascinating ways. When faced with high-stakes situations, our amygdala, the brain's emotional center, can trigger the fight-or-flight response, potentially clouding our judgment at precisely the moments when we need clarity most. This biological response, while useful for our ancient ancestors fleeing predators, requires careful management in the modern consulting environment.

The Anatomy of Consulting Pressure

Consulting pressure manifests in various forms, each requiring a unique approach to management. Client expectations often form the foundation of this pressure. Unlike regular corporate roles, where performance metrics are typically internal, consultants face the added complexity of external scrutiny. Every recommendation, analysis, and presentation is subject to intense examination by clients who have invested significant resources in seeking your expertise.

Consider the case of Marcus Chen, a consultant working on a critical healthcare transformation project. The pressure he faced wasn't just about meeting deadlines. It was about making recommendations that would affect patient care outcomes, staff satisfaction, and the hospital's financial sustainability. This multilayered pressure required him to develop a systematic approach to handling stress while maintaining peak performance.

The pressure in consulting often has a unique temporal characteristic: It's both immediate and future-oriented. You're not just solving today's problems; you're helping shape strategies that will impact organizations for years to come. This dual-timeline pressure requires consultants to develop what I call "temporal resilience," the ability to handle immediate stress while maintaining a clear long-term perspective.

Building Your Pressure Resilience Framework

Developing pressure resilience isn't about becoming immune to stress. It's about building a framework that allows you to function optimally under varying degrees of pressure. This framework begins with self-awareness. Understanding your pressure triggers, stress responses, and optimal performance conditions is crucial for managing high-stakes situations effectively.

The Pressure Resilience Framework consists of several interconnected elements:

- Cognitive Conditioning: Training your mind to maintain clarity under pressure involves regular exposure to challenging situations in controlled environments. This might include taking on increasingly complex projects, participating in high-stakes presentations, or leading difficult client conversations. The key is gradual exposure that builds confidence without overwhelming your capacity to cope.

- Physical Foundation: The mind-body connection plays a crucial role in pressure management. Regular exercise, proper sleep hygiene, and nutrition form the bedrock of pressure resilience. Many top consultants maintain strict physical routines not just for health but as a crucial element of their pressure management strategy.

The Art of Emotional Regulation

In the consulting world, emotional regulation becomes as important as technical expertise. The ability to maintain composure while dealing with challenging clients, tight deadlines, and complex problems sets exceptional consultants apart from average ones. This skill isn't about suppressing emotions. It's about understanding and channeling them effectively.

Take the experience of Diana Rodriguez, a partner at Boston Consulting Group. During a particularly challenging merger project, she faced intense opposition from key stakeholders. Instead of allowing the emotional tension to affect her judgment; she developed what she calls the "emotional stepping stone" approach—using emotional awareness as a tool for better decision-making rather than seeing it as an obstacle to overcome.

The process of emotional regulation in consulting involves several key components:

- **Recognition:** Developing the ability to identify emotional responses in real-time, understanding their triggers, and acknowledging their presence without judgment.
- **Analysis:** Evaluating the impact of emotional states on decision-making and performance, considering both short-term and long-term implications.
- **Response:** Implementing appropriate strategies to manage emotional states while maintaining professional effectiveness.

Strategic Pressure Management in Client Engagements

The art of managing pressure in client engagements requires a sophisticated understanding of both human psychology and business dynamics. When James Wilson, a senior partner at Bain & Company, faced a critical situation with a retail client undergoing digital transformation, he demonstrated how strategic pressure management could turn a potential crisis into an opportunity. The client's aggressive timeline and ambitious goals created immense pressure, but Wilson's approach showcased the elements of masterful pressure management in consulting.

Pressure in client engagements often manifests through multiple channels simultaneously. There's the explicit pressure of deliverables and deadlines but also the implicit pressure of maintaining relationships, managing expectations, and ensuring long-term value creation. Understanding these pressure points allows consultants to develop targeted strategies for each dimension.

The Science of Decision-Making Under Pressure

The consulting environment demands rapid, high-quality decision-making under significant pressure. Research in cognitive psychology reveals that pressure affects our decision-making processes in predictable ways.

227

Understanding these patterns helps consultants develop strategies to maintain optimal performance even in high-stress situations.

The brain's prefrontal cortex, responsible for executive functions like planning and decision-making, can become compromised under extreme pressure. This biological reality requires consultants to develop specific cognitive strategies to maintain clear thinking. The implementation of structured decision-making frameworks becomes crucial in these moments.

Consider the case of Elena Petrova, who developed a systematic approach to pressure-induced decision-making while working on a critical aerospace industry project. Her method, which she calls the "Pressure-Proof Protocol," involves breaking down complex decisions into manageable components and applying specific analytical tools to each element.

Building Team Resilience

Individual pressure management, while crucial, is only part of the equation. In consulting, success often depends on the collective resilience of project teams. Building team resilience requires a deliberate approach to creating supportive structures and processes that help teams thrive under pressure.

The concept of "distributed resilience" becomes particularly important in consulting teams. This approach recognizes that different team members have varying pressure thresholds and stress responses. By understanding and leveraging these differences, teams can create dynamic support systems that maintain high performance under pressure.

Communication Under Pressure

Effective communication becomes even more critical under pressure. The ability to convey complex ideas clearly and maintain productive dialogue when stakes are high often determines project success. This requires developing what I term "pressure-resistant communication skills" techniques that remain effective even under intense stress.

The elements of pressure-resistant communication include:

- **Clarity in Crisis:** Maintaining clear, concise communication even when time is limited and stakes are high. This involves developing the ability to distill complex information into digestible formats without losing crucial details.

- **Emotional Intelligence in Action:** Reading and responding to emotional undercurrents in high-pressure situations while maintaining professional composure. This skill becomes particularly important when dealing with stressed clients or team members.

Creating Sustainable High Performance

The challenge in consulting isn't just about managing pressure in isolated instances. It's about creating sustainable high performance over the long term. This requires developing what I call the "Pressure Equilibrium System," a balanced approach to maintaining peak performance while preventing burnout.

The Architecture of Mental Toughness

Developing mental toughness in consulting requires more than just resilience; it demands a structured approach to building psychological strength. The consulting environment, with its constant challenges and high expectations, necessitates what I call the "Consultant's Mental Architecture," a framework for maintaining peak performance under sustained pressure.

Time-Pressure Mastery

The relationship between time and pressure in consulting creates unique challenges. Tight deadlines, multiple concurrent projects, and the need for rapid yet thorough analysis can create a perfect storm of pressure. Developing mastery over time-pressure situations involves understanding the psychology of time perception and implementing strategic approaches to time management.

Victoria Chang, a partner at a leading consulting firm, developed the "Time Compression Technique," a method for maintaining quality while working under extreme time constraints. This approach involves identifying critical decision points and creating predetermined response frameworks for common time-pressure scenarios.

Crisis Management and Recovery

Even the most prepared consultants encounter crises. The key lies not just in managing these crises but in developing robust recovery mechanisms. This includes understanding the psychological impact of high-pressure failures and creating structured approaches to bouncing back stronger.

The "Post-Pressure Recovery Protocol" involves:

- Systematic analysis of pressure points

- Implementation of targeted recovery strategies
- Development of enhanced resilience through learned experiences

The Future of Pressure Management in Consulting

As the consulting industry evolves, new forms of pressure emerge. The digital transformation of consulting practices, increasing client expectations, and the globalization of services create novel challenges. Future-focused pressure management strategies must account for these emerging realities.

Integration of Technology and Human Resilience

The modern consultant must balance technological capabilities with human resilience. This involves understanding how to leverage technology to reduce certain pressures while maintaining the human elements that make consulting effective.

Maintaining Work-Life Harmony

The sustainable management of pressure requires a holistic approach to work-life harmony. This involves creating boundaries while maintaining flexibility, developing support systems, and implementing regular renewal practices.

The Evolution of Professional Resilience

As the consulting landscape continues to evolve, professional resilience must adapt accordingly. This includes developing new skills, embracing emerging technologies, and maintaining core psychological strength.

The Path Forward

Thriving under pressure in consulting isn't just about survival – it's about transformation. By developing comprehensive pressure management strategies, consultants can turn high-pressure situations into opportunities for growth and excellence.

The journey to mastering pressure in consulting is ongoing. It requires continuous learning, adaptation, and refinement of strategies. As the consulting world evolves, so too must our approaches to handling pressure, always maintaining the balance between performance and sustainability.

Owl-like Tactics for Managing Challenging Client Relationships

Understanding the Owl's Perspective

Like an owl perched high in its tree, successful consultants must develop a broader perspective when dealing with challenging clients. This elevated viewpoint allows for a better understanding of client behaviors, motivations, and underlying concerns that may not be immediately apparent.

The owl's ability to rotate its head 270 degrees mirrors the consultant's need to examine client relationships from multiple angles. This comprehensive view enables consultants to anticipate potential conflicts, identify root causes of tension, and develop proactive solutions before issues escalate.

The Silent Observer Strategy

Just as owls are masters of silent observation, successful consultants excel at reading client dynamics without immediate intervention. This involves:

Active Listening: Developing the ability to hear not just what clients say but what remains unsaid. Pay attention to tone, body language, and contextual clues that might indicate underlying concerns or resistance.

Pattern Recognition: Identifying recurring behaviors or situations that trigger client tension allows for preemptive action rather than a reactive response.

Nocturnal Navigation

Like owls navigating in darkness, consultants must often work through unclear or ambiguous client situations. This requires:

- Developing keen instincts for detecting early warning signs of client dissatisfaction
- Building trust through consistent, reliable performance
- Maintaining professional boundaries while showing genuine concern for client success

The Sharp-Eyed Approach

An owl's exceptional vision translates to a consultant's ability to spot both opportunities and potential problems in client relationships. This involves:

- **Detailed Observation:** Carefully monitor client interactions, team dynamics, and project progress to identify areas of potential friction.
- **Strategic Foresight:** Anticipating client needs and concerns before they become issues, allowing for proactive solution development.

Silent Flight Techniques

Just as owls fly silently to maintain effectiveness, consultants must learn to navigate difficult client situations without creating additional disturbance. This includes:

- **Diplomatic Communication:** Mastering the art of addressing sensitive issues without triggering defensive responses.
- **Conflict De-escalation:** Developing techniques to calm tense situations while maintaining project momentum.

The Wisdom Factor

The owl's association with wisdom translates to:

- **Experience Utilization:** Drawing from past experiences to inform current client relationship management strategies.
- **Knowledge Application:** Applying industry insights and best practices to strengthen client relationships.

Territorial Management

Like owls defending their territory, consultants must:

- **Establish Clear Boundaries:** Setting and maintaining professional limits while remaining flexible enough to accommodate reasonable client needs.

- **Protect Professional Standards:** Maintaining high-quality work and ethical practices even when under pressure from difficult clients.

The Hunter's Precision

An owl's precise hunting ability parallels a consultant's need for:

- **Accurate Problem Identification:** Pinpointing exact sources of client dissatisfaction or conflict.
- **Targeted Solutions:** Developing specific, customized approaches for each challenging client situation.

Adaptability in Different Environments

Just as owls adapt to various habitats, consultants must:

- **Adjust Communication Styles:** Modifying approaches based on client culture and preferences.
- **Develop Cultural Intelligence:** Understanding and respecting different organizational cultures and working styles.

Building Long-term Resilience

Like owls maintaining their territory over time, consultants must:

- **Develop Sustainable Relationships:** Creating lasting client partnerships that can weather occasional difficulties.

- **Maintain Professional Growth:** Continuously improving relationship management skills through experience and learning.

PART 5: CONTINUOUS LEARNING & FUTURE THINKING

CHAPTER 9
REFLECTION: THE OWL'S
MIRROR

The essence of wisdom lies not just in action but in reflection. Owls, often associated with wisdom, are revered for their calm demeanor and their ability to observe and learn from their surroundings. Similarly, the life of a management consultant is punctuated with challenges, victories, and setbacks. These moments, when mirrored with thoughtful reflection, become the foundation for growth, adaptability, and success. Reflection is not just a passive act; it is an active strategy, a deliberate pause to extract lessons from experiences, both good and bad. In this chapter, we delve into the art of reflective practice and how it can transform a consultant into a "360-degree Wise Owl."

The Power of Reflection in Management Consulting

Every consulting project has a unique journey from inception to closure. Yet, the most overlooked part of the process often lies at the end: reflection. Consultants are trained to move swiftly from one engagement to the next. Still, without stepping back to evaluate what went well and what could have been better, they risk repeating the same mistakes or missing opportunities to improve.

Reflection gives consultants the chance to refine their craft. It is not about obsessing over errors or basking in success but about extracting actionable insights from experiences. Think of it as polishing the "owl's mirror." The more you polish it, the clearer the image becomes, revealing strengths, weaknesses, and areas for growth.

For consultants, every engagement offers a mirror to see their approach more clearly. Did the strategy meet the client's needs? Were there gaps in communication? Could the execution have been smoother? Answering these questions objectively is the key to building resilience and skill over time.

Learning from Success: Celebrating Wins with Wisdom
Success is a double-edged sword. While it provides confidence and validation, it can also breed complacency. In consulting, success stories often serve as case studies for future clients. However, it is equally important to reflect on

the journey to success. What decisions led to the positive outcome? What risks were mitigated? Which strategies worked better than expected?

Take, for instance, a project where a consultant helped a manufacturing company streamline its operations, reducing costs by 20%. On the surface, this is a great achievement, but reflection can dig deeper:

- How did the consultant identify the inefficiencies?
- What methods of collaboration with the client's team worked best?
- Were there any risks that could have derailed the project but didn't?

Celebrating wins is important, but doing so with humility and curiosity enhances long-term expertise. Success is not the end; it is an opportunity to prepare for the next challenge with a sharper edge.

Learning from Failure: The Courage to Face the Mirror
While success provides confidence, failure offers lessons that success often cannot. Owls, as patient predators, occasionally miss their prey. Yet, they do not stop hunting. Instead, they learn from their missteps and recalibrate their

strategy. For management consultants, failure is an inevitable part of the journey. Projects may not meet their objectives, clients may feel unsatisfied, or strategies might fall short of expectations.

Failure can be painful to confront, but it is also where the deepest learning occurs. Reflecting on failure requires courage, a willingness to set ego aside, and an honest evaluation of what went wrong.

- Was the project scope miscalculated?
- Were the client's expectations misunderstood?
- Did internal communication gaps lead to inefficiencies?

True growth lies in accepting responsibility without defensiveness. Rather than seeing failure as a setback, view it as a stepping stone. Every seasoned consultant has a story of a project gone awry, and more often than not, these stories are the ones that taught them resilience, adaptability, and empathy.

Building a Reflective Practice in Consulting

Reflection is not a one-time activity but a habit that must be cultivated. Just as an owl instinctively surveys its surroundings, a consultant must build a routine of self-assessment and introspection. Here's how:

1. Post-Engagement Reviews

After the completion of every project, set aside time for a thorough review. Involve your team, if applicable, and discuss:

- What went well?
- What could have been improved?
- Were there any unexpected challenges, and how were they handled?

The goal is not to point fingers but to gain collective insights that can benefit future projects.

2. Personal Journaling

Maintaining a journal is a powerful way to capture reflections in real time. Jot down key moments from meetings, breakthroughs during brainstorming sessions, and lessons from client interactions. Over time, this journal becomes a treasure trove of wisdom.

3. Seeking Feedback

Reflection should not be a solitary exercise. Seek feedback from colleagues, mentors, and even clients. Often, an external perspective can shed light on blind spots you might have missed.

4. Continuous Learning

Reflection and learning go hand in hand. Enrol in workshops, read case studies and attend industry events. Use these experiences to cross-check your reflections against broader industry practices.

The Emotional Side of Reflection

Reflection is not purely analytical; it is also deeply emotional. Consulting can be a high-pressure career, filled with long hours, demanding clients, and tough decisions. Amid this chaos, reflection serves as a tool for emotional balance. It allows consultants to process frustrations, celebrate small victories, and stay connected to their purpose.

For example, if a project becomes particularly draining, reflecting on the "why" behind your work can rekindle motivation. Why did you choose to consult? What impact do you hope to create for your clients? These reflective questions bring clarity and re-align consultants with their values.

Becoming the 360-Degree Wise Owl

The ultimate goal of reflection is to achieve a 360-degree view of your consulting practice. Like the owl, which can rotate its head to see the world from all angles, a reflective consultant gains a holistic understanding of their work. This includes:

- **Seeing the bigger picture:** Understanding how individual projects contribute to long-term career goals.
- **Recognizing patterns:** Identifying recurring challenges and finding ways to address them.
- **Anticipating the future:** Using past experiences to predict and prepare for upcoming trends in the consulting world.

Sustaining Reflection: Turning Lessons into Action

Reflection, while invaluable, achieves its true purpose when it leads to actionable change. Owls, known for their adaptability, refine their hunting tactics based on their experiences. Similarly, a management consultant must not only learn from their reflections but also implement those lessons in their work. The act of turning insight into action is where growth truly begins.

Reflection as a Continuous Loop

Reflection is not a one-and-done activity. It must become an ongoing process embedded in your consulting practice. This continuous loop involves observing, analyzing, learning, and applying. Each project feeds into the next, creating a cycle of constant improvement.

For example, imagine a consultant who struggles with project timelines. Reflection reveals that delayed client feedback often derails progress. Turning this insight into action might involve building more structured client check-ins or adding buffer time in project plans. The next project will benefit from this adjustment, and the reflection cycle will continue with new challenges and solutions.

Balancing Confidence with Humility

Reflection offers an opportunity to balance confidence and humility. Reflecting on successes reinforces your strengths and builds your self-assurance. Reflecting on failures keeps you grounded and reminds you of the importance of continuous learning. This balance is essential for any consultant aiming to build a long-lasting career.

Overconfidence can blind a consultant to potential risks, while excessive humility might lead to self-doubt. By reflecting regularly, you learn to walk this fine line with grace. For instance, acknowledging that you successfully negotiated a challenging client contract is a confidence boost. However, recognizing that the process took longer than expected due to a lack of preparation keeps you striving for better.

Case Study: A Consultant's Journey in Reflection

To illustrate the power of reflection, let's consider the story of Sarah, a mid-level consultant at a boutique firm specializing in healthcare. Early in her career, Sarah faced a major setback: a hospital system she worked with decided to cancel their engagement midway through the project, citing dissatisfaction with the deliverables.

At first, Sarah was defensive, blaming the client for unclear expectations. However, after some guidance from her mentor, she decided to reflect more deeply on the situation. She identified several key issues:

- The initial project scope was not thoroughly aligned with the client's goals.
- Sarah's team failed to communicate regularly with the client, leading to misaligned expectations.

248

- She relied heavily on standardized solutions instead of tailoring strategies to the client's unique challenges.

Sarah used these insights to adjust her approach. She developed a more robust scoping process, created a system for regular client updates, and began taking the time to understand each client's needs deeply. Six months later, she landed a major project with another healthcare system and implemented these changes. Not only was the project successful, but the client extended their contract for an additional year.

This case highlights that setbacks are not the end of the road; they are opportunities to pause, reflect, and recalibrate.

The Role of Team Reflection in Consulting

While individual reflection is crucial, team reflection amplifies its impact. Consulting projects often involve collaboration, and a collective reflective practice can strengthen team dynamics and enhance project outcomes.

Consider incorporating team reflection sessions at key milestones during a project:

- **Mid-Project Check-Ins:** Discuss what's working and what needs adjustment. These discussions can prevent issues from escalating.
- **End-of-Project Reviews:** Analyze the entire engagement as a team. What were the highlights? Where were the pain points? How can the team work more effectively in the future?

Team reflection fosters transparency and trust. It allows every member to contribute their perspective, leading to richer insights. Additionally, it builds a culture of accountability, where success is shared, and lessons from mistakes are openly acknowledged.

Reflection and the Consultant-Client Relationship

Reflection does not have to be limited to internal practices. Consultants who involve their clients in reflective exercises strengthen their relationships and demonstrate a commitment to continuous improvement.

For example, at the end of a project, consider conducting a formal debrief with your client. Ask them questions like:

- What aspects of the project exceeded their expectations?
- Were there any areas where they felt underserved?

- How could the partnership be improved for future engagements?

These conversations show clients that you value their feedback and are invested in delivering the best possible outcomes. Additionally, client reflections often provide insights that you might not have considered, offering a fresh perspective on your consulting approach.

Using Reflection to Navigate Change

The consulting landscape is constantly evolving. New industries emerge, technologies disrupt traditional practices, and client needs shift with economic trends. In this environment, reflection becomes a vital tool for adaptability.

For instance, consider the rapid rise of artificial intelligence and its impact on business operations. A reflective consultant might ask:

- How is AI reshaping the industries I work with?
- Are there skills I need to develop to stay relevant in this new landscape?
- How can I incorporate AI-driven solutions into my consulting practice?

By regularly reflecting on external changes, consultants can stay ahead of the curve and position themselves as valuable, forward-thinking advisors to their clients.

Reflection as a Career Compass

Beyond its immediate benefits, reflection serves as a compass for long-term career development. Management consulting is a demanding field, and it is easy to lose sight of your personal goals amidst the hustle. Regular reflection helps you pause and ask:

- Am I aligned with my career aspirations?
- Do the projects I take on align with my values and passions?
- Am I investing in skills and experiences that will help me grow?

For example, if you consistently take on operational projects but your passion lies in strategy, reflection can help you recognize this misalignment and take steps to redirect your focus.

Honing the Owl's Mirror

The process of reflection is much like polishing a mirror. It takes effort, consistency, and patience, but the rewards are profound. A polished mirror reveals the full spectrum of who you are as a consultant: your strengths, your areas for growth, and your potential to make an impact.

The Emotional Depth of Reflection: Connecting Head and Heart

Reflection in consulting is often viewed through a technical lens, analyzing strategies, assessing performance, and refining processes. However, it also has an equally significant emotional dimension. Consulting can be a rollercoaster, filled with moments of triumph and frustration. By addressing the emotional side of reflection, consultants can achieve not just professional growth but personal resilience as well.

At its core, reflection invites you to connect your head (logic) with your heart (emotion). It's about acknowledging the human side of the consulting journey: the pressures of meeting client demands, the thrill of delivering results, and the self-doubt that can creep in during setbacks. Embracing these emotions and understanding their role in your experiences can lead to a more holistic sense of growth.

For example, if a particularly demanding client engagement leaves you feeling drained, reflect not only on the project's logistical challenges but also on how it affected your well-being. This type of emotional reflection can help you identify boundaries you need to set in the future or self-care practices to prioritize during high-pressure projects.

The Spiritual Side of Consulting: Purpose-Driven Work

Reflection can also lead consultants to grapple with deeper questions:

- Why do I do what I do?
- Am I making a meaningful impact?
- How does my work align with my values?

These questions tap into the spiritual side of consulting the quest for purpose and fulfillment. While day-to-day tasks may revolve around deliverables and deadlines, stepping back to reflect on your "why" can bring renewed clarity and motivation.

Take the example of a consultant who specializes in helping non-profits optimize their operations. While the technical side of the work involves cost analysis and efficiency metrics, the emotional and spiritual side is about contributing to causes that make a difference in the world. Reflecting on the impact of your work, not just for the client but for the broader community, can reignite your passion and provide a deeper sense of satisfaction.

Tools for Deep Reflection

To truly embrace reflection as a consultant, it helps to have a structured approach. Here are some tools and techniques to deepen your reflective practice:

1. The Reflection Grid

Create a simple grid with four sections:

- **What went well:** Identify successes and strengths.
- **What didn't go well:** Acknowledge setbacks without judgment.
- **What I learned:** Extract insights from both successes and failures.
- **What I'll do differently:** Define actionable steps for improvement.

This grid offers a balanced view of your experiences and serves as a guide for future engagements.

2. Storytelling as Reflection

Narrating your experiences, whether to a mentor, a colleague, or even in a journal, helps you process them more deeply. Storytelling brings clarity to complex situations, highlights key takeaways, and often reveals insights that may not surface in analytical reflection alone.

3. Mindfulness Practices

Incorporate mindfulness techniques such as meditation or deep breathing into your reflection routine. These practices create mental space, allowing you to approach reflection with a calm and focused mind. Mindfulness also enhances self-awareness, a critical skill for any consultant.

4. Vision Boards for Career Reflection

Visualizing your long-term goals through a vision board can be a powerful way to align your reflections with your aspirations. Add images, quotes, and symbols that represent your career goals, and use your reflections to track progress toward those goals.

The Legacy of a Reflective Consultant

As consultants progress in their careers, their reflections evolve from being project-specific to encompassing broader themes, such as leadership, mentorship, and legacy. Reflection at this stage is no longer just about personal growth; it becomes about the impact you leave behind.

A reflective consultant considers:

- **Mentorship:** How can I pass on the lessons I've learned to the next generation of consultants?
- **Client Relationships:** How can I build partnerships that leave a lasting positive impact?
- **Industry Contributions:** How can my work help shape the consulting profession for the better?

This shift from self-focused reflection to outward-focused reflection is the hallmark of a true "Wise Owl." It signifies the transition from skilled practitioner to trusted advisor, mentor, and leader.

The Reflective Consultant's Creed

To close this chapter, let's encapsulate the essence of reflection in a simple creed, a set of guiding principles for every consultant striving to polish their "owl's mirror":

- **Embrace curiosity:** Approach every experience as an opportunity to learn, whether it ends in success or failure.
- **Seek clarity:** Reflect not just on what happened but on why it happened and how it can inform future decisions.
- **Honor emotion:** Acknowledge the highs and lows of consulting as integral parts of the journey.
- **Take action:** Use insights from reflection to drive meaningful change in your work.

- **Share wisdom:** Pay forward the lessons you've learned to enrich the consulting profession.

A Lifelong Journey of Reflection

Reflection is not a destination; it is a lifelong journey. Like the owl that continuously hones its hunting skills, a consultant must remain committed to learning, adapting, and growing. Each project, each client, and each challenge adds a new layer of insight to the reflective mirror.

CHAPTER 10
THE FUTURE OF CONSULTING

The world of consulting has always been dynamic, shaped by economic shifts, technological advancements, and the changing demands of industries. Today, as we stand at the intersection of technological revolutions and global transformations, the consulting profession must evolve in tandem. In this chapter, we explore the future of consulting through the lens of the **"Wise Owl,"** a metaphor for adaptability, wisdom, and foresight qualities that will be essential for navigating the industry's future.

The **Wise Owl** model emphasizes the importance of being observant, insightful, and strategic in a constantly shifting field. Consulting professionals must not only anticipate trends but also learn to adapt, innovate, and lead their clients into an era marked by rapid technological change, environmental concerns, and increasingly complex global systems.

The Role of Technology in Shaping Consulting

Technology is no longer just a tool; it is the driving force behind transformation in nearly every industry. For consultants, technology offers both opportunities and challenges. Artificial intelligence (AI), machine learning, blockchain, and data analytics have not only reshaped how organizations operate but also how consultants approach their work.

The consulting landscape of tomorrow will require professionals to harness the power of technology to deliver value in innovative ways. In this context, the Wise Owl represents the ability to integrate technology into strategy without losing the human touch that is central to client relationships.

Automation and the Changing Nature of Work

Automation is eliminating repetitive and mundane tasks, freeing consultants to focus on strategic thinking and creative problem-solving. While this shift is advantageous, it also demands upskilling and a deeper understanding of emerging technologies. Management consultants must become fluent in tools like AI-powered analytics platforms, which can process data faster and more accurately than ever before.

But adaptability is key. Consultants must ask themselves: How can I stay ahead of the curve and deliver insights that machines alone cannot? This question reflects the owl's ability to adapt its hunting strategies based on its environment, a parallel for how consultants should operate in a technologically driven world.

AI as a Partner, Not a Replacement

Contrary to the fear that AI might replace consultants, the future suggests a more collaborative role for artificial intelligence. AI can handle massive datasets, identify patterns, and generate insights, but consultants must interpret and contextualize this information for their clients. AI excels at logic and prediction, but it lacks the empathy and strategic nuance that only human consultants can provide.

The wise consultant, like the Wise Owl, uses AI as an ally, leveraging its capabilities to deepen insights, improve efficiency, and enhance decision-making. The key lies in balancing the computational power of machines with the emotional intelligence and wisdom of human expertise.

The Owl's Eye: Seeing Opportunities in Industry Evolution

One of the owl's most remarkable features is its ability to see clearly, even in the darkest conditions. For consultants, this means identifying opportunities in the face of uncertainty. The industries of the future, ranging from renewable energy to biotechnology, will require a fresh perspective and a proactive approach.

Sustainability and ESG Consulting

As businesses face mounting pressure to align with environmental, social, and governance (ESG) standards, the demand for sustainability-focused consulting will grow exponentially. Clients will seek guidance on reducing carbon footprints, improving supply chain transparency, and meeting global sustainability goals. This shift represents a significant opportunity for consultants to redefine value creation.

The Wise Owl approach encourages consultants to think holistically. How does a company's sustainability strategy tie into its broader goals? How can ESG initiatives drive profitability while addressing societal challenges?

Consultants who can answer these questions will remain indispensable in the future marketplace.

The Rise of Hybrid Consulting Models

The consulting profession is also seeing the emergence of hybrid models, combining traditional advisory services with hands-on implementation. Clients are no longer satisfied with theoretical strategies; they want actionable solutions and measurable results. This trend aligns with the owl's balanced approach to observing, analyzing, and acting.

Hybrid consulting requires a deeper commitment to client success. Consultants must move beyond offering advice to becoming active partners in execution, leveraging digital tools and collaborative platforms to ensure long-term outcomes.

The Consultant, as a Lifelong Learner

In a rapidly changing world, the consultant of the future must embody the spirit of lifelong learning. Like the Wise Owl, which constantly hones its instincts and skills, consultants must remain curious and open to new ideas.

Upskilling and Reskilling for a Dynamic Industry

The skill sets that define successful consultants today may not suffice tomorrow. As technology evolves, so too must the capabilities of those who advise organizations on navigating change. Data science, coding, and digital marketing are just a few of the areas where consultants may need to develop expertise to stay relevant.

But technical skills alone are not enough. Emotional intelligence, cross-cultural communication, and creative thinking will be equally important in a future where global collaboration and diverse perspectives are key to solving complex problems.

Building Resilience in a Time of Disruption

Resilience is another hallmark of the Wise Owl. For consultants, this means developing the ability to weather industry disruptions, whether they stem from economic downturns, geopolitical conflicts, or unforeseen crises like pandemics. Resilient consultants are those who can pivot quickly, adapt their strategies, and maintain a forward-looking perspective.

Preparing for the Future: The Wise Owl's Toolkit

To thrive in the consulting industry of tomorrow, professionals must equip themselves with a robust toolkit that integrates wisdom, strategy, and adaptability. This toolkit includes:

- **Visionary Thinking**: The ability to anticipate future trends and align strategies with emerging opportunities.
- **Client-centric Innovation**: A commitment to tailoring solutions that meet unique client needs while leveraging cutting-edge technology.
- **Ethical Leadership**: Guiding clients toward decisions that are not only profitable but also socially and environmentally responsible.
- **Global Perspective**: Embracing diverse viewpoints and understanding the interconnectedness of global systems.

Embracing Technological Trends Without Losing the Human Touch

As the consulting industry leans further into technology, one critical factor remains irreplaceable: the human element. While technology drives efficiency, automation, and scalability, consulting is ultimately about people understanding their needs, solving their challenges, and building trust. The consultants of the future must master the art of blending technology with emotional intelligence, ensuring that solutions are not only efficient but also empathetic.

Data-Driven Decision-Making in Consulting

Data has become the lifeblood of modern businesses, and consultants who can transform raw data into actionable insights will be invaluable. Advanced analytics tools allow consultants to dissect market trends, identify patterns, and predict outcomes with precision. However, the true skill lies in interpreting these insights and weaving them into a coherent narrative that resonates with clients.

The Wise Owl reminds us that data is only as powerful as the story it tells. A consultant's ability to contextualize numbers and connect them to real-world implications will be a defining trait in the future. Whether it's helping a company expand into a new market or refine its operational strategy, data-backed storytelling will be a key differentiator.

Augmented Reality and Virtual Reality in Consulting

Emerging technologies like augmented reality (AR) and virtual reality (VR) are opening new doors for consultants, especially in training, customer experience design, and operational simulations. Imagine a consultant using VR to immerse a client in a simulated environment, enabling them to visualize the outcomes of a strategic decision before it's implemented. These technologies make consulting not only more interactive but also more precise in delivering value.

Still, the consultant must maintain a human-centered approach. While AR and VR provide tools for visualization, consultants must guide clients through the emotional and strategic implications of their choices, ensuring alignment with organizational goals.

Adapting to Globalization and Cross-Cultural Collaboration

The future of consulting will be increasingly global. Companies operate in interconnected markets, where decisions made in one region have ripple effects across the globe. Consultants must be prepared to navigate the complexities of global business, from cross-cultural communication to geopolitical risks.

The Consultant as a Cultural Bridge

A single ecosystem does not bind the Wise Owl; it thrives in diverse environments. Similarly, consultants of the future must embrace cultural diversity, recognizing that what works in one region may not translate seamlessly to another. This requires a deep understanding of cultural nuances, local market dynamics, and regional regulatory frameworks.

For example, a consultant advising a multinational corporation on market entry into Asia must consider cultural factors like consumer behavior, negotiation styles, and governmental policies. Success hinges not only on strategic insight but also on cultural sensitivity.

Remote Collaboration and the Digital Nomad Consultant

The COVID-19 pandemic accelerated the shift toward remote work, and this trend is here to stay. In the consulting industry, this means more virtual client interactions, remote project teams, and cross-border collaborations. Consultants who can build relationships and maintain productivity in a virtual environment will have a competitive edge.

The Wise Owl's adaptability is a useful metaphor here: just as the owl adjusts its hunting patterns to suit its environment, consultants must embrace new ways of working, leveraging digital tools to maintain efficiency and rapport. Platforms like Zoom, Slack, and Microsoft Teams are no longer optional; they are essential for maintaining connectivity in a dispersed workforce.

Sustainability as a Core Consulting Focus

Sustainability is no longer a buzzword. It's a necessity. Governments, investors, and consumers are demanding that businesses operate responsibly, balancing profit with purpose. For consultants, this represents a significant opportunity to shape the future of industries by integrating sustainability into strategic planning.

Circular Economy and Green Innovation

One area where consultants can add immense value is in helping clients transition to a circular economy. This involves designing business models that minimize waste, maximize resource efficiency, and create long-term value. Consultants can guide companies in adopting practices like recycling, reusing materials, and developing eco-friendly products.

Green innovation is another growing field. From renewable energy to carbon capture technologies, businesses are investing heavily in sustainable solutions. The Wise Owl's approach here is one of foresight; consultants must not only understand the current sustainability landscape but also anticipate future trends and guide their clients accordingly.

Measuring and Communicating ESG Impact

Consultants are increasingly tasked with helping organizations measure their ESG (Environmental, Social, and Governance) impact and communicate it effectively to stakeholders. This requires expertise in data collection, reporting frameworks, and storytelling. Investors and consumers want transparency, and consultants play a crucial role in helping companies build trust through honest and impactful ESG reporting.

Consulting in a World of Disruption

Disruption has become the new normal, with industries regularly facing challenges like economic instability, geopolitical tensions, and technological breakthroughs. The consultants of the future must not only respond to disruption but also anticipate it, positioning themselves as trusted advisors in times of uncertainty.

Scenario Planning and Risk Management

Scenario planning will be a cornerstone of future consulting engagements. This involves mapping out multiple potential futures and helping clients prepare for each one. For instance, a consultant working with an automotive company might explore scenarios related to the rise of electric vehicles, regulatory changes, or supply chain disruptions.

Risk management will also take center stage. From cyber security threats to global health crises, consultants must help organizations build resilience by identifying vulnerabilities and creating robust contingency plans. The Wise Owl's ability to see in the dark reminds us of the importance of clarity and preparedness in the face of uncertainty.

Building Agility in Organizations

Agility is no longer just a buzzword; it's a survival skill. Organizations that thrive in a disrupted world are those that can pivot quickly, embrace change, and innovate continuously. Consultants play a vital role in fostering this agility, whether by redesigning processes, encouraging a culture of innovation, or introducing agile methodologies.

The Wise Owl's balance of patience and quick reflexes is an apt metaphor here. Consultants must strike a balance between thoughtful planning and rapid execution, ensuring that their clients are equipped to navigate change effectively.

Looking Ahead: The Legacy of the Wise Owl

As we conclude this exploration of the future of consulting, it's clear that a combination of technology, globalization, sustainability, and disruption will shape the industry's evolution. The Wise Owl serves as a powerful symbol for the qualities that consultants must embody to thrive in this environment: wisdom, adaptability, and foresight.

The Evolution of the Consultant's Role

As industries transform, the role of the consultant must also evolve. No longer is it enough to provide expert advice from the sidelines. Clients expect consultants to immerse themselves in their challenges, deliver actionable solutions, and drive measurable results. This evolution demands a shift in how consultants position themselves—not just as advisors but as collaborators and catalysts for change.

From Problem Solver to Change Maker

In the past, consultants were primarily viewed as problem solvers brought in to address specific challenges or inefficiencies. However, the future consultant must go beyond this transactional role. The **Wise Owl** embodies the qualities of a change maker: someone who doesn't just react to problems but proactively identifies opportunities and crafts transformative strategies.

This means engaging with clients at a deeper level and understanding their vision, culture, and long-term objectives. Consultants must become partners in innovation, co-creating solutions that not only resolve immediate issues but also position the organization for sustained success. This shift requires a combination of analytical rigor, emotional intelligence, and the ability to inspire confidence in the face of uncertainty.

The Rise of Purpose-Driven Consulting

Modern businesses are increasingly aligning their strategies with broader societal goals, such as inclusivity, sustainability, and ethical leadership. As a result, consultants must adopt a purpose-driven approach, helping clients align their operations with their values. This goes beyond profitability to encompass the organization's impact on employees, communities, and the planet.

The future consultant must be able to authentically and confidently navigate this shift toward purpose. Like the Wise Owl, which observes its surroundings holistically, consultants must help clients see the bigger picture, ensuring that their strategies create value for all stakeholders, not just shareholders.

Technology as an Enabler, Not a Replacement

While technological advancements will continue to shape the consulting industry, they should be viewed as enablers rather than replacements. Tools like AI, data analytics, and machine learning can enhance efficiency and provide deeper insights, but they cannot replace the intuition, creativity, and interpersonal skills that define effective consulting.

Building Trust in the Age of Technology

As technology becomes more pervasive, maintaining trust will become a critical challenge. Clients will look to consultants not only for technical expertise but also for ethical guidance in navigating complex issues like data privacy, AI ethics, and digital transformation. The Wise Owl's wisdom reminds us that trust is built through transparency, integrity, and a commitment to doing what's right.

For example, when advising a client on implementing AI solutions, a consultant must not only consider the technical feasibility but also the ethical implications. How will the technology impact employees? Are there biases in the algorithms that need to be addressed? By asking these questions and guiding clients toward responsible practices, consultants can position themselves as trusted advisors in an increasingly tech-driven world.

The Importance of Relationships in the Digital Era

Even as technology reshapes the consulting landscape, relationships will remain at the heart of the profession. The ability to build and maintain strong client relationships will continue to be a key differentiator for successful consultants.

Cultivating Long-Term Partnerships

In the future, consultants will need to focus on building long-term partnerships rather than short-term engagements. This requires a deep understanding of the client's business, industry, and unique challenges. It also demands ongoing communication and a commitment to delivering value over time.

The Wise Owl's patience and loyalty remind us of the importance of trust and consistency. By investing in relationships and demonstrating a genuine commitment to their client's success, consultants can establish themselves as indispensable allies.

Balancing Digital Interactions with Human Connection

The rise of remote work and digital collaboration tools has transformed how consultants interact with clients. While these technologies offer convenience and efficiency, they also risk eroding the personal connection that is so vital to effective consulting. The future consultant must find ways to balance digital interactions with meaningful human connections.

For example, while virtual meetings and emails may suffice for routine updates, in-person interactions will remain crucial for building rapport, resolving complex issues, and fostering trust. The Wise Owl's ability to adapt to its environment reminds us that consultants must be flexible in their approach, choosing the right tools and methods for each situation.

Preparing for the Unknown: The Consultant's Mindset

The only certainty about the future is that it will be unpredictable. For consultants, this means developing a mindset that embraces uncertainty and views change as an opportunity rather than a threat.

Cultivating a Growth Mindset

A growth mindset is essential for thriving in an industry that is constantly evolving. This mindset involves viewing challenges as opportunities for learning, seeking out feedback, and continuously improving one's skills. The Wise Owl's curiosity and adaptability inspire this mindset, reminding us that wisdom is not static but ever-growing.

Consultants with a growth mindset are more likely to innovate, take calculated risks, and lead their clients through uncharted territory. Whether it's exploring new technologies, entering unfamiliar markets, or tackling complex social issues, a willingness to learn and evolve will be key to staying relevant.

The Power of Reflection

In the fast-paced world of consulting, it's easy to get caught up in the day-to-day demands and lose sight of the bigger picture. The Wise Owl's contemplative nature reminds us of the importance of reflection. Taking time to evaluate past projects, learn from successes and failures, and refine one's approach is crucial for long-term growth.

Consultants can incorporate reflection into their routine by regularly reviewing their performance, seeking feedback from clients and colleagues, and staying informed about industry trends. This practice not only enhances individual effectiveness but also contributes to the overall success of consulting teams and organizations.

CONCLUSION
THE 360° WISE OWL MINDSET

This journey through **The Future of Consulting** has illuminated one undeniable truth: the world of consulting is in a state of constant transformation, and success lies in the ability to adapt, innovate, and inspire. At the core of this transformation is the **360° Wise Owl mindset**, a philosophy that encapsulates the qualities every consultant must embody to thrive in an ever-evolving landscape.

The **360° Wise Owl** is more than a metaphor. It is a call to action. It symbolizes the balance between analytical precision and emotional intelligence, the harmony of foresight and adaptability, and the ability to see both the broader picture and the intricate details. This mindset is a compass for navigating the complexities of modern consulting, guiding professionals toward a future defined by impact, purpose, and progress.

The Pillars of the Wise Owl Mindset

As we reflect on this guide, the core principles of the Wise Owl mindset emerge clearly:

- **Wisdom:** The ability to draw on experience, knowledge, and insight to offer solutions that resonate deeply with clients' needs.
- **Adaptability:** A willingness to evolve, embrace change, and pivot in the face of new challenges and opportunities.
- **Strategy:** The skill to craft actionable, forward-thinking plans that align with a client's vision and goals.
- **Empathy:** Recognizing that consulting is, at its heart, a people-centered profession, one that requires understanding, compassion, and collaboration.
- **Vision:** The capacity to see beyond the present, anticipating future trends, disruptions, and opportunities to lead clients toward sustainable success.

These principles form the foundation of the Wise Owl mindset, a framework that enables consultants to excel in their roles and create lasting value for their clients, their teams, and the industries they serve.

Inspiring Consultants to Embrace Wisdom and Adaptability

The consulting profession is not for the faint of heart. It demands resilience, curiosity, and a relentless pursuit of excellence. Yet, it is also a deeply rewarding field, one that allows professionals to solve complex problems, shape the future of businesses, and leave a meaningful impact on the world.

To truly thrive, consultants must go beyond simply acquiring skills or mastering tools; they must embrace the essence of the Wise Owl. This means approaching every challenge with an open mind, seeking to learn from every experience, and striving to create solutions that balance pragmatism with purpose.

In the face of uncertainty, the Wise Owl offers a beacon of clarity and confidence. Its 360° perspective reminds us to consider every angle, anticipate the ripple effects of our decisions, and remain steadfast in our commitment to excellence. Just as the owl is known for its ability to see in the dark, consultants must navigate uncharted territories with poise and precision, guiding their clients through challenges and helping them uncover opportunities they might not have seen.

A Vision for the Future

The consulting industry is at a crossroads, with technology, globalization, and sustainability reshaping its landscape. For those willing to rise to the occasion, this is not a time to fear change but to embrace it. The Wise Owl mindset equips consultants to meet the future head-on, armed with the tools, insights, and adaptability needed to lead in an era of transformation.

Let this serve as an invitation to all consultants aspiring, current and future, to embody the spirit of the Wise Owl. Be curious yet deliberate. Be strategic yet empathetic. Above all, be adaptable and always ready to evolve with the times. By doing so, you will not only succeed in your career but also contribute to shaping a consulting industry that is innovative, impactful, and deeply aligned with the values of wisdom and progress.

The journey of the Wise Owl is a lifelong one, much like the journey of a consultant. The future will undoubtedly bring challenges, but it will also bring opportunities to innovate, connect, and inspire. Embrace the mindset, embody the wisdom, and become the consultant who sees the world not just as it is but as it could best.

Acknowledgements

This book would not have been possible without the contributions, expertise, and unwavering support of the following individuals and organizations. I extend my deepest gratitude to:

Alexandra Kim

A distinguished economist known for her groundbreaking research on global financial markets. Her insights into economic trends have greatly influenced my understanding of financial systems.

Andrew Chen

A leading software engineer known for developing AI-driven financial models that revolutionized algorithmic trading in 2022.

Andrew Glen

A renowned data scientist whose work in artificial intelligence and predictive analytics has shaped modern financial technology. His guidance on data-driven decision-making has been invaluable.

Boston Consulting Group

One of the world's leading management consulting firms, recognized for its strategic business solutions and industry-leading research. Their reports and frameworks have provided essential perspectives for this book.

David Morrison

A distinguished economist who played a key role in drafting the 2020 global economic recovery plan following the COVID-19 pandemic.

Deloitte

One of the world's largest professional services firms, instrumental in advising governments and corporations during the 2008 financial crisis.

Dr. Amanda Thompson

A celebrated neuroscientist and author whose research on cognitive behavior and decision-making has deeply enriched discussions on human psychology in finance.

Dr. Elena Rodriguez

A renowned medical researcher who led groundbreaking studies in genetic therapies, earning the 2023 Global Health Innovation Award.

Dr. Jennifer Liv

A medical innovator and entrepreneur whose work in biotechnology has transformed patient care. Her contributions to the intersection of health and finance have been inspiring.

Dr. Marcus Chen

A pioneering neuroscientist credited with discovering key mechanisms behind neuroplasticity, leading to major advancements in cognitive rehabilitation in 2021.

Dr. Richard Torres

A respected climate scientist and sustainability advocate, whose research on environmental economics has been crucial in exploring the financial impact of climate change.

Dr. Sarah Hayes

An influential public health expert who was at the forefront of global vaccination campaigns during the 2020-2022 pandemic.

James Mitchell

A technology strategist and venture capitalist who has played a key role in fostering innovation in fintech startups. His expertise in emerging technologies has shaped many discussions in this book.

Maria Stevenson

A leading advocate for financial literacy and inclusion, whose work has helped bridge the gap between complex financial concepts and everyday decision-making.

Mark Stevens

A venture capitalist known for funding early-stage technology startups, including a major role in the rise of quantum computing firms in 2024.

Michael Chen

A cybersecurity specialist who developed a breakthrough encryption protocol in 2023, strengthening global digital security.

Michael O'Connor

A respected historian whose research on 19th-century economic policies reshaped modern financial regulations in 2022.

Patrick Zhao

A global investment expert known for his leadership in asset management and risk analysis. His expertise in market trends has been instrumental in refining investment strategies discussed here.

Rachael Martinez

A distinguished journalist and investigative reporter covering business and finance. Her ability to distill complex financial topics into accessible narratives has been a great inspiration.

Sarah Chen

A renowned entrepreneur and business leader, whose advocacy for women in leadership and innovation has been a driving force in fostering inclusive financial growth.

Sarah Thompson

A bestselling author and journalist recognized for her investigative reporting on corporate ethics, which led to significant industry reforms.

Victoria Wu

A legal expert specializing in corporate law and financial regulation. Her insights into financial compliance and ethical investing have greatly informed key sections of this book.

To all of you, I extend my heartfelt appreciation for your contributions, expertise, and support throughout this journey. Sincere apologies if you were missed.

Printed in Great Britain
by Amazon